PRESIDENT'S MALARIA INITIATIVE

Kenya

Malaria Operational Plan FY 2016

TABLE OF CONTENTS

ABBREVIATIONS and ACRONYMS.. **3**

I. EXECUTIVE SUMMARY... **4**

II. STRATEGY **8**

1. Introduction.. 8
2. Malaria situation in Kenya.. 9
3. Country health system delivery structure and Ministry of Health (MoH) organization............... 11
4. National malaria control strategy.. 13
5. Updates in the strategy section 15
6. Integration, collaboration, and coordination 15
7. PMI goal, objectives, strategic areas, and key indicators 18
8. Progress on coverage/impact indicators to date... 20
9. Other relevant evidence on progress 21
10. Challenges and opportunities 21

III. OPERATIONAL PLAN **24**

1. Insecticide-treated nets... 24
2. Indoor residual spraying... 28
3. Malaria in pregnancy... 31
4. Case management.. 34
5. Health system strengthening and capacity building... 46
6. Behavior change communication.. 51
7. Monitoring and evaluation 54
8. Operational research.. 59
9. Staffing and administration... 62
   Table 1: Budget Breakdown by Mechanism FY 2016..................................... 63
   Table 2: Budget Breakdown by Activity FY 2016 65

ABBREVIATIONS and ACRONYMS

ACSM	Advocacy communication and social mobilization
AL	Artemether-lumefantrine
ACT	Artemisinin-based combination therapy
ANC	Antenatal care
BCC	Behavior change communication
CDC	Centers for Disease Control and Prevention
CHEW	Community health extension worker
CHMT	County health management team
CHV	Community health volunteer
DfID	U.K. Department for International Development
DHS	Demographic and Health Survey
DMSC	Drug Management Subcommittee
EPI	Expanded Program on Immunization
FELTP	Field Epidemiology and Laboratory Training Program
FY	Fiscal year
Global Fund	Global Fund to Fight AIDS, Tuberculosis and Malaria
GoK	Government of Kenya
IEC	Information, education, communication
IPC	Interpersonal communication
IPTp	Intermittent preventive treatment for pregnant women
IRS	Indoor residual spraying
ITN	Insecticide-treated mosquito net
KEMSA	Kenya Medical Supply Agency
KMS	Kenya Malaria Strategy 2014–2018
M&E	Monitoring and evaluation
MEDS	Mission for Essential Drugs
MIP	Malaria in pregnancy
MIS	Malaria Indicator Survey
MoH	Ministry of Health
MOP	Malaria Operational Plan
MQM	Medicines quality monitoring
NMCP	National Malaria Control Program
NQCL	National Quality Control Laboratory
NGO	Non-governmental organization
PMI	President's Malaria Initiative
PPB	Pharmacy and Poisons Board
QoC	Quality of Care (survey)
RDT	Rapid diagnostic test
RMNH	Reproductive Maternal Newborn Health
SCHMT	Sub-county health management team
SP	Sulfadoxine-pyrimethamine
UNICEF	United Nations Children's Fund
USAID	United States Agency for International Development
USG	United States Government
WHO	World Health Organization

I. EXECUTIVE SUMMARY

When it was launched in 2005, the goal of the President's Malaria Initiative (PMI) was to reduce malaria-related mortality by 50% across 15 high-burden countries in sub-Saharan Africa through a rapid scale-up of four proven and highly effective malaria prevention and treatment measures: insecticide-treated mosquito nets (ITNs); indoor residual spraying (IRS); accurate diagnosis and prompt treatment with artemisinin-based combination therapies (ACTs); and intermittent preventive treatment for pregnant women (IPTp). With the passage of the Tom Lantos and Henry J. Hyde Global Leadership against HIV/AIDS, Tuberculosis, and Malaria Act in 2008, PMI developed a U.S. Government Malaria Strategy for 2009–2014. This strategy included a long-term vision for malaria control in which sustained high coverage with malaria prevention and treatment interventions would progressively lead to malaria-free zones in Africa, with the ultimate goal of worldwide malaria eradication by 2040–2050. Consistent with this strategy and the increase in annual appropriations supporting PMI, four new sub-Saharan African countries and one regional program in the Greater Mekong Subregion of Southeast Asia were added in 2011. The contributions of PMI, together with those of other partners, have led to dramatic improvements in the coverage of malaria control interventions in PMI-supported countries, and all 15 original countries have documented substantial declines in all-cause mortality rates among children less than five years of age.

In 2015, PMI launched the next six-year strategy, setting forth a bold and ambitious goal and objectives. The PMI Strategy for 2015–2020 takes into account the progress over the past decade and the new challenges that have arisen. Malaria prevention and control remains a major U.S. foreign assistance objective and PMI's Strategy fully aligns with the U.S. Government's vision of ending preventable child and maternal deaths and ending extreme poverty. It is also in line with the goals articulated in the RBM Partnership's second generation global malaria action plan, *Action and Investment to Defeat Malaria (AIM) 2016-2030: for a Malaria-Free World* and WHO's updated *Global Technical Strategy: 2016-2030*. Under the PMI Strategy for 2015–2020, the U.S. Government's goal is to work with PMI-supported countries and partners to further reduce malaria deaths and substantially decrease malaria morbidity, towards the long-term goal of elimination.

Kenya was selected as a PMI focus country in FY 2007. This FY 2016 Malaria Operational Plan presents a detailed implementation plan for Kenya, based on the strategies of PMI and the National Malaria Control Program (NMCP). It was developed in consultation with the NMCP and with the participation of national and international partners involved in malaria prevention and control in the country. The activities that PMI is proposing to support fit in well with the National Malaria Control strategy and plan and build on investments made by PMI and other partners to improve and expand malaria-related services, including the Global Fund to Fight AIDS, Tuberculosis, and Malaria (Global Fund) malaria grants. This document briefly reviews the current status of malaria control policies and interventions in Kenya, describes progress to date, identifies challenges and unmet needs to achieving the targets of the NMCP and PMI, and provides a description of activities that are planned with FY 2016 funding.

The proposed FY2016 PMI budget for Kenya is $32.4 million. PMI will support the following intervention areas with FY 2016 funds:

Insecticide-treated nets (ITNs): Kenya seeks to achieve universal coverage with long-lasting ITNs, defined as one net per two people, in 23 endemic and epidemic-prone counties. In the rolling mass distribution campaign scheduled for 2014–2015, Kenya will distribute a total of 13.6 million ITNs. The first and second phases of the campaign took place in 6 counties in 2014 and distributed 3.3 million ITNs. The remainder of the nets will be distributed in 17 counties in 2015, including 3.8 million ITNs procured with PMI support. The other primary distribution strategy is free ITNs provided through antenatal care (ANC) and the Expanded Program on Immunization (EPI) clinics in 36 counties to ensure the most vulnerable populations are protected.

The FY 2016 funding will procure an estimated 1.5 million ITNs for free routine distribution through ANC and EPI clinics and an estimated 100,000 ITNs to support development of alternative continuous distribution channels and replacement strategies at the community level to meet and maintain universal coverage in one county following the planned 2017–2018 mass ITN campaign. Additionally, PMI will continue to work with implementing partners and local non-governmental organizations on community-based behavior change communication (BCC) programs to increase demand for ITNs and encourage correct and consistent use.

Indoor residual spraying (IRS): The NMCP's plan for IRS has been to spray in the lake-endemic counties of western Kenya; the target for IRS implementation is seven malaria-endemic counties in western Kenya with an estimated population of 8.7 million. PMI supported the national IRS program from 2008 to 2012. In 2012, PMI was the sole funder of IRS and over 2.4 million people were covered in parts of three counties with pyrethroid insecticide. No spraying took place from 2013–2015 due to the transition to a non-pyrethroid insecticide, a change rendered necessary by the emergence of insecticide resistance throughout much of western Kenya. The insecticide transition necessitated changes to national policy and registration of an alternative insecticide. The use of a more expensive non-pyrethroid insecticide will increase the cost of IRS.

With FY 2016 funding, PMI in collaboration with the NMCP will support IRS in up to one priority county. The estimated population coverage is over 1 million people. PMI will support entomological monitoring in counties with historical IRS programs as well as in counties where IRS is expected to resume in 2017.

Malaria in pregnancy (MIP): The national package of ANC services includes both malaria prevention and treatment interventions based on epidemiologic-risk zones. Free ITNs and malaria prevention BCC is provided for all pregnant women in 36 counties; IPTp with sulfadoxine-pyrimethamine (SP) is recommended (i.e., doses at all ANC visits after quickening and at least four weeks apart) is policy in the 14 counties with high malaria endemicity. All women attending ANC clinics are screened for anemia during the first and fourth visits, and all pregnant women with signs and symptoms consistent with malaria should receive a diagnostic test and prompt treatment if positive. Since 2011, PMI has provided support for MIP interventions at the national level including policy and messaging review, development and dissemination, procurement and distribution of ITNs through ANC clinics, and strengthening of case management. In the 14 malaria-endemic counties, PMI has provided support for the full package of MIP interventions, including IPTp.

With FY 2016 funding, PMI will support intensive MIP interventions in five malaria-endemic counties targeting health facilities with ANC services and an estimated 5,500 community health volunteers to reach an estimated 50,000 pregnant women to encourage early ANC attendance and receipt of the full package of prevention and case management services.

Case management: The *2014 National Guidelines for Diagnosis, Treatment and Prevention of Malaria in Kenya* recommend diagnosis with a parasitological test (i.e., microscopy or malaria rapid diagnostic test [RDT]) and first-line treatment with artemether-lumefantrine (AL) for uncomplicated malaria and parenteral artesunate for severe malaria. PMI has invested in malaria diagnostics, case management, and supply chain management strengthening. Since 2008, PMI has procured and distributed over 300 microscopes, almost 12.6 million RDTs, and supported strengthening of diagnostics by training over 4,700 healthcare workers. PMI has also procured almost 48 million AL treatments and distributed over 36.5 million and has trained over 5,000 healthcare workers on national case management guidelines.

With FY 2016 funding, PMI will support integrated strengthening of case management (i.e., strengthening diagnostic capacity and clinical case management proficiency together) at the health-facility, sub-county and county levels. PMI will procure and distribute approximately 8 million RDTs to help meet the projected national RDT gap based on testing of all suspected malaria. PMI will also procure and distribute approximately 4.5 million AL treatments to help meet the projected national AL gap and 500,000 vials of injectable artesunate to treat severe malaria and complement the funding for this medication from other partners and the Government of Kenya.

Health systems strengthening and capacity building: Since 2008, PMI has invested in efforts to build capacity and integrate with other programs across the health sector. PMI strengthens the overall health system by investing in human capacity through the Field Epidemiology and Laboratory Training Program to increase epidemiology capacity in the Ministry of Health, improving governance in the pharmaceutical sector including strengthening and expanding sentinel sites, Pharmacy and Poisons Board, and National Quality Control Laboratory to monitor medication quality, building capacity for health information systems, surveillance and monitoring and evaluation (M&E) across the health sector, strengthening commodity management systems, expanding access to and ensuring a reliable supply of essential medicines, and improving service delivery in the different intervention areas.

With FY 2016 funds, PMI will continue to support capacity building through short- and long-term training and mentoring and health systems strengthening for pharmaceutical regulation and monitoring, supply chain management, and health information utilization at the national level. However, PMI will increasingly direct its focus and resources to the county level.

Behavior change communication (BCC): Through community mobilization, interpersonal communication, and use of national, county, and local mass media to disseminate key messages and encourage positive health-seeking behavior, PMI has promoted correct and consistent ITN use, prompt diagnosis and treatment for fever, and demand for community and facility-based case management and MIP services since 2008. Since 2013, PMI has supported intensive community-based interpersonal communication (IPC) at the household level via local community organizations and community health volunteers (CHVs) to reach the highest-risk populations in high-burden malaria counties with historically low intervention uptake.

With FY 2016 funding, PMI will continue to support cross-cutting BCC investments at community, sub-county, county, and national levels, with a particular emphasis on working with community-based local organizations to strengthen and target IPC activities at the household and village levels to at-risk and hard-to-reach populations.

Monitoring and evaluation (M&E): PMI provides support to the NMCP to ensure that critical gaps in the revised *Kenya Malaria Strategy Monitoring and Evaluation Plan 2014–2018* are funded. PMI has supported M&E capacity needs assessments at the national and county levels, development and implementation of a malaria surveillance curriculum to improve routine malaria surveillance data, development and production of quarterly malaria surveillance bulletins, national annual malaria reports, biannual Quality of Care (QoC) surveys, and data quality audits in priority counties to standardize malaria data collection and reporting.

With FY 2016 funding, PMI will concentrate support at the national level on specific gaps identified in M&E capacity and in M&E Plan activities, expand support for capacity building at the county level based on identified needs, and continue support for monitoring of interventions through the biannual QoC surveys, therapeutic efficacy and ITN field durability activities.

Operational Research (OR): PMI supports the NMCP's strategic OR activities that are in line with PMI's OR priorities list. PMI has supported a wide range of OR activities across the focus areas including vector control, case management, and malaria in pregnancy. There are ongoing OR studies but no new OR studies planned with FY 2016 funding.

II. STRATEGY

1. Introduction

When it was launched in 2005, the goal of PMI was to reduce malaria-related mortality by 50% across 15 high-burden countries in sub-Saharan Africa through a rapid scale-up of four proven and highly effective malaria prevention and treatment measures: insecticide-treated mosquito nets (ITNs); indoor residual spraying (IRS); accurate diagnosis and prompt treatment with artemisinin-based combination therapies (ACTs); and intermittent preventive treatment for pregnant women (IPTp). With the passage of the Tom Lantos and Henry J. Hyde Global Leadership against HIV/AIDS, Tuberculosis, and Malaria Act in 2008, PMI developed a U.S. Government Malaria Strategy for 2009–2014. This strategy included a long-term vision for malaria control in which sustained high coverage with malaria prevention and treatment interventions would progressively lead to malaria-free zones in Africa, with the ultimate goal of worldwide malaria eradication by 2040–2050. Consistent with this strategy and the increase in annual appropriations supporting PMI, four new sub-Saharan African countries and one regional program in the Greater Mekong Subregion of Southeast Asia were added in 2011. The contributions of PMI, together with those of other partners, have led to dramatic improvements in the coverage of malaria control interventions in PMI-supported countries, and all 15 original countries have documented substantial declines in all-cause mortality rates among children under five years of age.

In 2015, PMI launched the next six-year strategy, setting forth a bold and ambitious goal and objectives. The PMI Strategy for 2015–2020 takes into account the progress over the past decade and the new challenges that have arisen. Malaria prevention and control remains a major U.S. foreign assistance objective and PMI's Strategy fully aligns with the U.S. Government's vision of ending preventable child and maternal deaths and ending extreme poverty. It is also in line with the goals articulated in the RBM Partnership's second generation global malaria action plan, *Action and Investment to Defeat Malaria (AIM) 2016-2030: for a Malaria-Free World* and WHO's updated *Global Technical Strategy: 2016-2030*. Under the PMI Strategy for 2015–2020, the U.S. Government's goal is to work with PMI-supported countries and partners to further reduce malaria deaths and substantially decrease malaria morbidity, towards the long-term goal of elimination.

Kenya was selected as a PMI focus country in FY 2007.

This FY 2016 Malaria Operational Plan presents a detailed implementation plan for Kenya, based on the strategies of PMI and the National Malaria Control Program (NMCP) strategy. It was developed in consultation with the NMCP and with the participation of national and international partners involved in malaria prevention and control in the country. The activities that PMI is proposing to support fit well with the National Malaria Control strategy and plan and build on investments made by PMI and other partners to improve and expand malaria-related services, including the Global Fund to Fight AIDS, Tuberculosis, and Malaria (Global Fund) grants. This document briefly reviews the current status of malaria control policies and interventions in Kenya, describes progress to date, identifies challenges and unmet needs to achieving the targets of the NMCP and PMI, and provides a description of activities that are planned with FY 2016 funding.

2. Malaria situation in Kenya

Kenya's 2013 population is estimated at 44.3 million people, with an estimated population growth of 2.7% per year; thus, Kenya's 2015 population is projected to be 46.7 million.[1] Of the total population, children under age five account for 16% and children under age 15 account for 42%.[1,2] Geographically, the country falls into two main regions: lowland areas, both coastal and around the Lake Victoria basin, and highland areas on both sides of the Great Rift Valley. Kenya has approximately 42 ethnic groups and is a predominantly agricultural economy with a strong industrial base. Kenya is ranked 147 out of 187 countries on the 2014 United Nation's Human Development Index, which measures life expectancy, adult literacy and per capita income.[3] Life expectancy in Kenya has seen an overall downward trend since the late 1980s but has recently increased to an estimated 62 years in 2013.[4] The HIV/AIDS estimated adult prevalence is 6%.[4] The total expenditure on health increased slightly from 4.1% of the gross domestic product in 2004 to 4.5% in 2013.[5] The Government of Kenya's (GoK) per capita health expenditures also rose from $19 in 2000 to $45 in 2013.[5] The mortality rate in children under five years of age has declined by 55% from 115 deaths per 1,000 live births in the 2003 Kenya Demographic and Health Survey (DHS) to 52 deaths per 1,000 observed in the 2014 DHS.[6, 7]

Malaria still remains a major public health problem in Kenya and accounts for an estimated 18% of outpatient consultations and 6% of hospital admissions based on data from the routine health information system.[8] Malaria transmission and infection risk in Kenya is determined largely by altitude, rainfall patterns, and temperature. Therefore, malaria prevalence varies considerably by season and across geographic regions. The variations in altitude and terrain create contrasts in the country's climate, which ranges from tropical along the coast to temperate in the interior to very dry in the north and northeast. There are two rainy seasons—the long rains occur from April to June and the short rains from October to December. The highest temperatures are from February to March and the lowest from July to August.

All four species of *Plasmodium* that infect humans occur in Kenya. *Plasmodium falciparum*, which causes the most severe form of the disease, is the most common accounting for over 99% of all malaria infections in the country. The major malaria vectors in Kenya are *An. gambiae* complex (*An. gambiae ss, An. arabiensis, An. merus*) and *An. funestus*. The malaria vector distribution in the country is not uniform due to variation in climatic factors, particularly temperature and rainfall.

About 80% of the Kenyan population is at risk for malaria.[9] Among the at-risk population, 27% (approximately 12 million people) live in areas of epidemic and seasonal malaria transmission where *P. falciparum* parasite prevalence is usually less than 5%. However, an estimated 28 million people live in

[1] World Bank, http://www.worldbank.org/en/country/kenya. Accessed 25 May 2015.

[2] UNICEF, State of the World's Children 2015, http://www.unicef.org/infobycountry/kenya_statistics html. Accessed 25 May 2015.

[3] United Nations Development Programme. Human Development Index Trends, 1980-2013, http://hdr.undp.org/en/content/table-2-human-development-index-trends-1980-2013. Accessed 25 May 2015.

[4] UNICEF. State of the World's Children 2015, http://www.unicef.org/infobycountry/kenya_statistics html. Accessed 25 May 2015.

[5] World Bank, http://data.worldbank.org/indicator/SH.XPD.PCAP/countries . Accessed 25 May 2015. [Public health expenditure consists of recurrent and capital spending from government (central and local) budgets, external borrowings and grants (including donations from international agencies and nongovernmental organizations) and social (or compulsory) health insurance funds.]

[6] Central Bureau of Statistics (CBS) [Kenya], Ministry of Health (MOH) [Kenya], and ORC Macro. 2004. *Kenya Demographic and Health Survey 2003*. Calverton, Maryland: CBS, MOH, and ORC Macro.

[7] Kenya National Bureau of Statistics (KNBS), Ministry of Health (MOH) [Kenya], and ICF International. 2015. *Kenya Demographic and Health Survey Key Indicators 2014*. Nairobi, Kenya: KNBS, MOH, and ICF International.

[8] Ministry of Health (MOH) [Kenya]. *Kenya Annual Malaria Report, 2013-2014 (Draft)*. In preparation.

[9] Noor AM, Kinyoki DK, Ochieng JO, Kabaria CW, Alegana VA, Otieno VA, Kiptui R, Soti D, Yé Y, Amin AA, Snow RW. The epidemiology and control profile of malaria in Kenya: reviewing the evidence to guide the future vector control. Nairobi: DOMC and KEMRI-Welcome Trust-University of Oxford-Research Programme, 2012.

endemic areas, and over a quarter (approximately 11 million people) live in areas where parasite prevalence is estimated to be equal to or greater than 20%. For the purposes of malaria control, the country has been stratified into four epidemiological zones to address the varied risks:

- **Endemic areas:** These areas of stable malaria have altitudes ranging from sea level in the coastal region to up to 1,300 meters around the Lake Victoria basin in western Kenya. Transmission is intense throughout the year with *P. falciparum* prevalence historically greater than 20% and high annual entomological inoculation rates. The coastal counties now have malaria prevalence ranging from 5–20%. Of the total population, 26% lives in a malaria-endemic zone.

- **Highland and epidemic-prone areas:** Malaria transmission in the western highlands is seasonal with considerable year-to-year variation. The entire population is vulnerable and case-fatality rates during an epidemic can be greater than in endemic regions. Approximately 39% of Kenyans live in these areas. The malaria prevalence in these areas ranges from 5–20%.

- **Seasonal malaria transmission areas:** This epidemiological zone includes the arid and semi-arid areas of northern and central parts of the country, which experience short periods of intense malaria transmission during the rainy seasons. Although the largest zone in terms of geographic size, only 14% of the population lives in areas where the malaria prevalence is between 1–5%.

- **Low malaria risk areas:** This zone covers the central highlands of Kenya including Nairobi. Approximately 21% of the population lives in this area.

Kenya's 2010 population-adjusted *P. falciparum* prevalence map (Figure 1) depicts the malaria prevalence by county with the highest *P. falciparum* prevalence in the lake-endemic counties represented by the darker shaded areas. The 2010 Malaria Indicator Survey (MIS) indicated that malaria prevalence in the western lake endemic zone, the darkest area of the map, remained very high at 38%.[10]

---

[10] Division of Malaria Control (DOMC) [Ministry of Public Health and Sanitation], Kenya National Bureau of Statistics (KNBS), and ICF Macro. *2010 Kenya Malaria Indicator Survey*. Nairobi: DOMC, KNBS and ICF Macro, 2011.

Figure 1. Map of Kenya: 2010 Population-adjusted *P. falciparum* Prevalence by County[11]

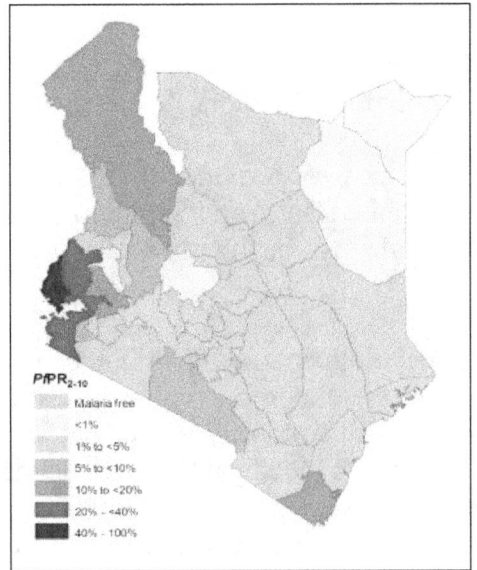

3. Country health system delivery structure and Ministry of Health (MoH) organization

Service delivery is provided along a continuum of care starting from the community level and ending at the country's national referral hospitals through a hierarchy of healthcare levels (Figure 2).

Figure 2. Service Delivery Pathway[12]

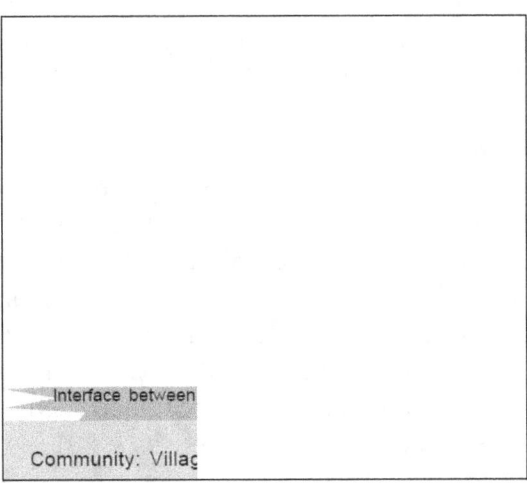

The national long-term development plan, *Kenya Vision 2030,* guides the country's strategies including the health sector. The Kenya Health Sector Strategic and Investment Plan (KHSSP) 2014–2018 provides a range of services and interventions that will be covered under this plan. These services are comprehensively defined under the Kenya Essential Package for Health Services. Malaria has been identified as a disease program area that contributes to the Kenya Essential Package for Health Services under the following policy objectives:

[11] Noor AM, Kinyoki DK, Ochieng JO, Kabaria CW, Alegana VA, Otieno VA, Kiptui R, Soti D, Yé Y, Amin AA, Snow RW. *The epidemiology and control profile of malaria in Kenya: reviewing the evidence to guide the future vector control.* Nairobi: DOMC and KEMRI-Welcome Trust-University of Oxford-Research Programme, 2012.
[12] KHSSP II 2005-2010

1. Accelerate the burden of reduction of communicable conditions
2. Reduce the burden of violence and injuries
3. Provide essential health services
4. Minimize exposure to health risk factors
5. Strengthen collaboration with health related sectors

From 2008–2013, health services in Kenya were provided through two ministries, the Ministry of Medical Services and the Ministry of Public Health and Sanitation. Following elections in 2013 and as part of the GoK reorganization process, the two health ministries were reunited as a single Ministry of Health (MoH).

In 2013, Kenya began the process of devolution as set forth in the 2010 Constitution of Kenya. The transition to 47 counties from 8 provinces as the primary administrative unit has a 3-year time line for full implementation guided by a Transitional Authority. At the national level, the MoH has a Cabinet Secretary, Principal Secretary, and Director of Medical Services. Under the Director of Medical Services are five directorates. The Directorate of Preventive and Promotive Services houses the Division of Communicable Disease Prevention and Control. The NMCP has been a part of the Division of Communicable Disease Prevention and Control since late 2013. Key functions at the national level include health policy, national referral health facilities and reference laboratories, disease surveillance, monitoring and evaluation, health commodity procurement for large donor-funded programs including malaria, capacity building and technical assistance.

The Transitional Authority, working together with Sectoral Function Assignment and Competency Teams, has established roles, responsibilities, and functions of the national and county governments. The changes have necessitated the re-alignment of PMI-supported interventions and implementation at the new administrative units in 2014 and beyond. The changes have had an impact on operational costs and human resources due to shifting roles, responsibilities, and functions.

National Malaria Control Program
The NMCP is currently staffed by technical professionals who are seconded from other divisions in the MoH. The unit has six technical teams: (1) vector control, (2) case management, (3) malaria in pregnancy, (4) epidemic preparedness and response, (5) advocacy, communication and social mobilization, and (6) surveillance, monitoring and evaluation (M&E), and operational research (OR). Each team has a focal point and one or more technical officers. The current structure and staff within the NMCP remains relatively intact compared to other units under the Division of Communicable Disease Prevention and Control. However, consolidation of technical teams, functions and reassignment of staff to counties or other programs has been an ongoing process since 2013.

The Malaria Interagency Coordination Committee (MICC) is convened biannually and on an *ad hoc* basis by the NMCP on behalf of the Director of Preventive and Promotive Services. The MICC includes other MoH divisions and units, non-governmental organizations, community-based organizations, private sector, partners and donors. The NMCP also has six primary technical working groups (TWGs) that meet quarterly and are aligned with the six technical teams. In addition, the primary TWGs have the capacity to form sub-committees for more concentrated discussion or work around a particular issue. The sub-committees report back through the primary working group structure. For example, the Advocacy, Communication, and Social Mobilization TWG started a Resource Mobilization sub-committee in 2013, and the Case Management TWG has standing Drug Management and Diagnostic sub-committees.

County Departments of Health
The counties have a health executive and a director for health, with oversight of the health management team. The health executive and director for health are appointed by the governor in each county. The health executive appointees are not necessarily from the health sector; the majority of county health directors are physicians. Each county health department should have four primary units including preventive and promotive services. The county malaria control program and malaria control coordinator should be part of preventive and promotive services. Functions important to malaria control programs that have been transferred to the counties include health services management, communicable and vector-borne disease control and management, and environmental health services. Health financing, health information systems and M&E are expected to be shared functions between the national and county levels. However, the structures and personnel are not yet fully in place in the counties to implement these functions effectively.

Devolution to county governments has impacted the NMCP and PMI. The administrative changes have impacted operational plans and costs as a result of new county-level health structures and malaria control programs. The program costs have increased as county health structures and malaria control programs have become functional and the NMCP continues to provide support to ensure continuity of operations and implementation of malaria interventions.

4. National malaria control strategy

The GoK remains committed to improving health service delivery and places a high priority on malaria prevention and control. The NMCP is currently in the process of a review and revision of the Kenya Malaria Strategy 2014–2018 (KMS) and is also currently revising the M&E Plan in accordance with the revised strategy. The NMCP has prioritized malaria prevention and treatment interventions and outlined them in the revised KMS 2014–2018, which has six strategic objectives that together are focused on reaching a two-third reduction of malaria morbidity and mortality by 2018 compared to 2009, the start date of the original strategy:

- **Objective 1:** To have at least 80% of people living in malaria-risk areas using appropriate malaria preventive interventions.

- **Objective 2:** To have 100% of fever cases which present to a health worker receive prompt and effective diagnosis and treatment.

- **Objective 3:** To ensure that 100% of malaria epidemic-prone and seasonal-transmission counties have the capacity to detect and the ability to respond to malaria epidemics.

- **Objective 4:** To ensure that all malaria surveillance, monitoring and evaluation, and program indicators are routinely monitored, reported, and evaluated in all counties.

- **Objective 5:** To increase utilization of all malaria control interventions by at-risk communities in Kenya to at least 80%.

- **Objective 6:** To improve capacity in coordination, leadership, governance and resource mobilization at all levels towards achievement of the malaria program objectives.

Strategies to support the achievement of the revised KMS objectives include adopting a multi-sectoral approach to malaria control, decentralizing malaria control operations to counties beginning in 2013, tailoring interventions to the prevailing epidemiology, and strengthening the malaria control performance monitoring and evaluation system. Given the varied and changing malaria epidemiology, Kenya is targeting appropriate intervention measures for specific malaria-risk areas. The NMCP has strategically reprioritized the approved malaria control interventions according to malaria risk, in order to target resources towards achieving the highest impact possible.

Kenya Malaria Strategy – strategic approach by intervention

Vector Control
The revised KMS set a target of 80% of the at-risk population using appropriate malaria prevention interventions, including ITNs and IRS by 2018. The GoK plans to achieve universal ITN coverage (i.e., one net for every two people) for all groups at in malaria-endemic and epidemic-prone counties through: (1) regular rolling mass ITN distribution campaigns, carried out every three years in targeted geographic areas (i.e., 23 counties); (2) routine distribution through antenatal care (ANC) and Expanded Programme on Immunization (EPI) clinics in 36 counties; (3) social marketing of nets particularly in designated rural counties; and (4) commercial sales of ITNs in the private sector. The revised KMS has prioritized IRS for malaria-endemic counties with additional support for capacity building and focal IRS in epidemic-prone counties.

Malaria in Pregnancy
The *2014 National Guidelines for the Diagnosis, Treatment and Prevention of Malaria in Kenya* emphasize the integration of MIP in the overall ANC package for maternal health that includes IPTp, ITNs, prompt diagnosis and treatment of fever due to malaria, and behavior change communication to promote early ANC attendance, ITN use and IPTp uptake. Sulfadoxine-pyrimethamine (SP) should be administered at each ANC visit after quickening at 4-week intervals under direct observation in the 14 moderate-to-high transmission counties.

Case Management
The revised KMS target for case management is to ensure that 100% of all suspected malaria cases receive a parasitological diagnosis by microscopy or malaria RDT and effective treatment with the first-line treatment, artemether lumefantrine (AL). Artesunate injection is recommended for pre-referral and treatment of severe malaria.

The KMS recommends that community health volunteers (CHVs) receive training and supportive supervision for case management of malaria, prevention, behavior change communication, record keeping and reporting. Both RDTs and AL will be integrated into the CHV kit, and all CHVs will be linked to the nearest health facility for resupply of commodities, supervision, monitoring and referral.

Advocacy, Communication and Social Mobilization
The national target is to strengthen advocacy, communication and social mobilization to increase utilization of all malaria control interventions by at-risk communities in Kenya to at least 80%. Implementation of behavior change communication (BCC) activities focus on the involvement of health providers and CHVs in malaria prevention and control activities. Additional emphasis will be placed on using interpersonal communication (IPC) approaches delivered by CHVs, community-based organizations and special interest groups to target hard-to-reach populations and deliver personalized

messaging. Traditional channels of communication (e.g., television, radio, print, mobile phones) will be used, particularly during the 2015 mass ITN campaign.

Surveillance, Monitoring and Evaluation, and Operational Research
Surveillance, monitoring and evaluation and operational research are vital for tracking the progress of malaria prevention and control activities. The NMCP has a comprehensive M&E Plan to accompany the revised KMS, which recommends the frequency and methodology of monitoring key program indicators for each of the interventions in order to assess and inform program implementation.

5. Updates in the strategy section

The key updates are related to a mid-term strategic review undertaken in 2014. The revision of the KMS and M&E plan was supported by United Kingdom's Department for International Development (DfID), the World Health Organization (WHO), PMI, and implementing partners.

- Revision of the Kenya Malaria Strategy 2014–2018 with updated time lines for indicators and incorporation of new roles and responsibilities following devolution. The revised KMS is expected to be finalized with costing in June 2015.

- Revision of the Kenya Malaria Strategy Monitoring and Evaluation Plan 2014–2018 with updated time lines for indicator performance. The revised M&E Plan is expected to be finalized with costing in June 2015.

The most recent Kenya Demographic and Health Survey (DHS) was conducted in 2014 with data collected at the national and county levels. The key indicator report was released in early 2015; the full report and data set are expected to be released by the end of 2015. Overall, child mortality and malaria indicators have improved compared to the 2010 Malaria Indicator Survey (MIS) and 2008–09 DHS.[13]

6. Integration, collaboration, and coordination

The U.S. Government team in Kenya has developed a strategy that embraces a whole-of-government, multi-layer communication strategy, reflecting all fundamental principles of PMI. The Department of Defense, Department of Health and Human Services/Centers for Disease Control and Prevention (CDC), Department of State, Peace Corps, U.S. Agency for International Development (USAID), and President's Emergency Plan for AIDS Relief (PEPFAR) have implemented and reported on a large program base for several years. This multi-tiered governance structure allows for full participation across agencies, at all levels, and across technical areas which has resulted in programming responsive to Kenya's needs. Examples include:

- The NMCP and PMI have worked closely with the Walter Reed Army Institute of Research's Malaria Diagnostics Center to support and strengthen malaria diagnostic capacity and implement a quality assurance/quality control (QA/QC) program for malaria diagnostics. PMI-supported activities have included the procurement and distribution of microscopes, malaria microscopy training, QA/QC officer training, development and production of the *National Guidelines on Parasitological Diagnosis of Malaria and Malaria Vector Surveillance in Kenya* (2013) and

---

[13] Kenya National Bureau of Statistics (KNBS), Ministry of Health (MOH) [Kenya], and ICF International. 2015. Kenya Demographic and Health Survey Key Indicators 2014. Nairobi, Kenya: KNBS, MOH, and ICF International.

accompanying microscopy wall charts and job aids, and implementation of the QA/QC program for malaria diagnostics in health facilities.

- The NMCP and PMI have partnered with Peace Corps since 2011 to support community-based malaria activities. PMI supported three trained malaria volunteers in 2013–2014 to mobilize volunteers across sectors to plan and incorporate malaria prevention and control activities in the communities where they live and work. However, in July 2014, Peace Corps withdrew all volunteers from Kenya due to security concerns.

- The NMCP and PMI have a long-standing relationship with the Kenya Medical Research Institute (KEMRI) through the KEMRI-CDC Public Health Collaboration and KEMRI-Wellcome Trust collaboration. KEMRI collaborative malaria research has contributed to the development of each of the pillars of malaria prevention and control (i.e., effective case management, IPTp, ITNs, and IRS). Current surveillance and OR activities are focused on epidemiological and entomological surveillance and new medications and treatment strategies to inform national policy, strategies and program implementation.

In addition to U.S. Government integration and collaboration, PMI facilitates coordination of activities among key malaria partners in Kenya, including Global Fund, DfID, Malaria Control and Elimination Partnership in Africa (MACEPA), WHO, United Nations Children's Fund (UNICEF), research institutions, non-governmental organizations, private sector, and other donors and stakeholders. PMI is an integral partner to the NMCP and actively participates in annual planning and reviews, technical working groups, interagency coordination committees, and other stakeholder-related activities.

To enhance the impact of PMI-funded activities and in coordination with the NMCP and key partners, PMI has transitioned to a more narrow geographic focus since 2013. PMI supports the distribution of malaria medications and RDTs, surveillance and M&E and behavior change communication nationally, consistent with NMCP/MOH policies and strategies. Per NMCP policy, SP for IPTp is distributed only in the 14 endemic counties of the coast and western Kenya regions. For the ITN program, PMI supports routine distribution via ANC and EPI clinics in 36 counties; for mass campaign distribution, a total of 23 counties receive nets, and PMI support is directed to 5 counties in the western Kenya region. The majority of other PMI activities, including programmatic support for strengthening case management and surveillance and M&E, IRS and MIP, are focused in the eight lake-endemic counties with the highest burden of malaria (Figure 1). A map showing the counties and the estimated malaria burden is paired with a table of PMI-supported activities by county and strategy to help visualize the geographic focus (Figure 3). In counties without PMI-focused support, the NMCP and other partners are leading malaria prevention and control activities.

Figure 3. Geographic Focus of PMI-supported Activities by County and Strategy[14]

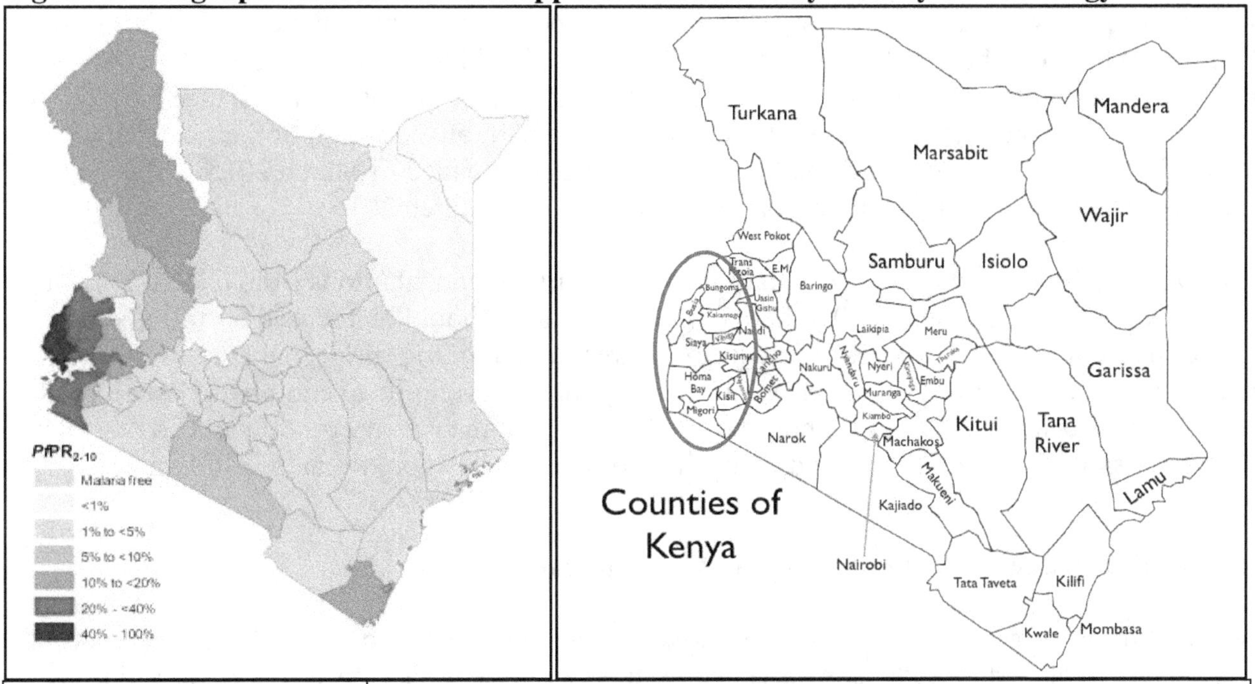

Transmission Zone	Counties (name or #)	Malaria Interventions					
		Case management	IPTp / MIP	ITNs (# of counties for routine distribution)	BCC	Surveillance + M&E	IRS
Lake endemic (red circle on map)	Migori	▓	▓	▓	▓	▓	▓
	Homa Bay	▓	▓	▓	▓	▓	
	Kisumu	▓	▓	▓	▓	▓	
	Siaya	▓	▓	▓	▓	▓	
	Busia	▓	▓	▓	▓	▓	
	Bungoma	▓	▓	▓	▓	▓	
	Kakamega	▓	▓	▓	▓	▓	
	Vihiga	▓	▓	▓	▓	▓	
Coast endemic	6			6			
Epidemic-prone highlands	11			10			
Seasonal	13			8			
Low-risk	9			4			

IPTp/MIP=intermittent preventive treatment in pregnancy/malaria in pregnancy; ITNs=insecticide-treated bed nets; BCC=behavioral change communication; M&E=monitoring and evaluation; IRS=indoor residual spraying with insecticides
Coding: white=no activities currently planned; gray shading=activities ongoing; hatched=PMI-supported activities ongoing

Financial support for the NMCP's plan has historically come from three primary sources: PMI, Global Fund, and DfID. The five-year Global Fund Round 10 grant, which runs from 2012–2016, has a value of $111 million or $22.3 million per year. The African Medical and Research Foundation (AMREF) received a concurrent five-year Global Fund Round 10 grant from 2012–2016. The AMREF grant of

---

[14] Noor AM, Kinyoki DK, Ochieng JO, Kabaria CW, Alegana VA, Otieno VA, Kiptui R, Soti D, Yé Y, Amin AA, Snow RW. The epidemiology and control profile of malaria in Kenya: reviewing the evidence to guide the future vector control. Nairobi: DOMC and KEMRI-Welcome Trust-University of Oxford-Research Programme, 2012.

$16 million supports implementation of community case management of malaria in the endemic counties of western Kenya. Historically, DfID has provided about half (approximately 1.2–1.4 million) of the ITNs for routine distribution through ANC and EPI/child health clinics and another 600,000-800,000 ITNs for social-marketing channels, support through WHO for technical assistance, surveillance, monitoring and evaluation, and OR, and $7 million for an extension of the Affordable Medicines Facility – malaria. However, the DfID malaria program ended in March 2015; DfID granted a one-year, no-cost extension for programming to partners through March 2016.

Based on the revised KMS strategy, budget analysis and confirmed contributions from Global Fund and DfID, PMI has concluded that the FY 2016 budget ($32.4 million) should be focused on filling critical program gaps, particularly commodities. The confirmed available funding (projected total of approximately $32.4 million in 2017, with PMI as the only major donor due to ending of Global Fund Round 10 grant in December 2016) to support the NMCP's annual malaria prevention and control plan falls significantly short of the expected need, which is estimated to be approximately $300 million annually.

7. PMI goal, objectives, strategic areas, and key indicators

Under the PMI Strategy for 2015–2020, the U.S. Government's goal is to work with PMI-supported countries and partners to further reduce malaria deaths and substantially decrease malaria morbidity, towards the long-term goal of elimination. Building upon the progress to date in PMI-supported countries, PMI will work with NMCPs and partners to accomplish the following objectives by 2020:

1. Reduce malaria mortality by one-third from 2015 levels in PMI-supported countries, achieving a greater than 80% reduction from PMI's original 2000 baseline levels.

2. Reduce malaria morbidity in PMI-supported countries by 40% from 2015 levels.

3. Assist at least five PMI-supported countries to meet the World Health Organization's (WHO) criteria for national or sub-national pre-elimination.[15]

These objectives will be accomplished by emphasizing five core areas of strategic focus:
   1. Achieving and sustaining scale of proven interventions
   2. Adapting to changing epidemiology and incorporating new tools
   3. Improving countries' capacity to collect and use information
   4. Mitigating risk against the current malaria control gains
   5. Building capacity and health systems towards full country ownership

To track progress toward achieving and sustaining scale of proven interventions (area of strategic focus #1), PMI will continue to track the key indicators recommended by the Roll Back Malaria Monitoring and Evaluation Reference Group (RBM MERG) as listed below:

- Proportion of households with at least one ITN
- Proportion of households with at least one ITN for every two people
- Proportion of children under five years old who slept under an ITN the previous night
- Proportion of pregnant women who slept under an ITN the previous night
- Proportion of households in targeted districts protected by IRS

---

[15] http://whqlibdoc.who.int/publications/2007/9789241596084_eng.pdf

- Proportion of children under five years old with fever in the last two weeks for whom advice or treatment was sought
- Proportion of children under five with fever in the last two weeks who had a finger or heel stick
- Proportion receiving an ACT among children under five years old with fever in the last two weeks who received any antimalarial drugs
- Proportion of women who received two or more doses of IPTp for malaria during ANC visits during their last pregnancy

8. Progress on coverage/impact indicators to date

Table 1: Evolution of Key Malaria Indicators in Kenya from 2003 to 2014

Indicator	2003, DHS[a]	2007, MIS[b]	2008–09, DHS[c]	2010, MIS	2014, DHS
% Households with at least one ITN	6%	48%	56%	48%	59%
% Households with at least one ITN for every two people	N/A	N/A	N/A	N/A	34%
% Children under five who slept under an ITN the previous night	5%	39%	47%	42%	54%
% Pregnant women who slept under an ITN the previous night	4%	40%	49%	41%	51%
% Households in targeted districts protected by IRS	N/A	N/A	N/A	26%[d]	N/A
% Children under five years old with fever in the last two weeks for whom advice or treatment was sought	74%	70%[e]	N/A	59%	72%
% Children under five with fever in the last two weeks who had a finger or heel stick	N/A	N/A	N/A	12%	35%
% Children receiving an ACT among children under five years old with fever in the last two weeks who received any antimalarial drugs	N/A	N/A	N/A	51%	86%
% Women who received two or more doses of IPTp during their last pregnancy in the last two years	4%	13%	15%	25%	36%[f]
% Children aged 6-59 months with a hemoglobin measurement of <8 g/dL	N/A	4%	N/A	5%	N/A
% Children aged 6-59 months with malaria infection[g]	N/A	3%	N/A	8%	N/A

[a] Pre-PMI baseline data for all-cause under-five mortality
[b] PMI baseline data for coverage indicators
[c] PMI baseline data for all-cause under-five mortality
[d] In epidemic-prone highlands and lake-endemic areas targeted for IRS
[e] Indicator: percentage of children under five years old with fever who sought treatment from a facility or health provider the same or next day
[f] In the 14 endemic counties with an IPTp policy; national estimate was 17%
[g] By microscopy

9. Other relevant evidence on progress

In mid-2014, DfID funded a nationally-representative survey as part of an end-of-project evaluation for their bilateral ITN and BCC programs.[16] Over 6,300 households were sampled for ITN indicators and over 8,000 households were sampled for BCC indicators. The key ITN finding was that access to nets, defined by attaining universal coverage at the household level, is directly associated with use of nets by both children under five years of age and all household members. In households that met universal coverage (i.e., having at least one ITN for every two people), 87% of children under five years of age slept under an ITN the previous night compared to 49% in households without universal coverage. In the endemic lake and coastal regions, where children are at highest risk for malaria, 89–96% of children under five years of age slept under an ITN the previous night in households with universal coverage. The results of the survey indicate that by simply increasing the number of nets within a household to ensure universal coverage, the targets for ITN usage could be met.

The key BCC findings were that exposure to both mass media and IPC were strongly associated with ITN use among all household members. Mass media was defined as malaria messaging via radio and television, and IPC was defined as any form of interpersonal communication or educational outreach such as malaria messaging during home visits by CHVs or other health workers, small group health sessions, and road and market shows. For households with exposure to mass media and at least one net, 91% of children under five years of age slept under an ITN the previous night compared to 78% without mass media exposure (p=0.001). For households with exposure to IPC and at least one net, 88% of children under five years of age slept under an ITN the previous night compared to 81% without IPC exposure (p=0.002). Only 36% of respondents reported IPC exposure compared to 83% of respondents reporting mass media exposure. The results of the survey indicate that BCC is reaching the target audience and positively influencing ITN use. Although good penetration is reported for mass media campaigns, scale up of IPC has not been achieved.

10. Challenges and opportunities

Within the context of devolution, ensuring that county governments prioritize and finance malaria prevention and control interventions is a primary challenge. Salaries for healthcare workers comprise over 70% of the health budget for most counties. The community health strategy was devolved to the counties, and currently, only one malaria-endemic county is funding CHV stipends. The other counties are relying on partners to fund the community strategy, and as a result, most counties have only partially implemented the strategy and stipends are inconsistent across partner programs.

In addition, the Kenya Medical Supply Agency (KEMSA) has transitioned from a traditional central medical store using a push-distribution system to a parastatal with a self-sustaining business model to provide commodities and services to clients (e.g., the national government, county governments, donors) using a fee-for-service pull-distribution system. The transition has resulted in frequent stockouts and erratic supplies of both RDTs and AL to health facilities because counties have limited capacity to quantify needs and insufficient budgets, and KEMSA has been unable to maintain a full pipeline of commodities to meet county needs. The NMCP and KEMSA have had to implement a "smart push" system for donor-funded malaria commodities to prevent irrational procurements and widespread stockouts at the health-facility level. The lack of a consistent malaria commodity supply has contributed

---

[16] Aloo, S. Findings of the 2014 malaria TRaC study among populations living in different malarial zones of Kenya. Presented at: National Malaria Control Program Monitoring and Evaluation Technical Working Group Meeting; 2014 December 3; Nairobi, Kenya.

to delays in implementation of the malaria community case management strategy because health facilities are either reluctant to give limited commodities to CHVs or have no commodities to supply CHVs. Working with counties to prioritize and finance health commodities and service delivery will be essential to safeguard the gains made nationally in malaria case management during this transition period.

The loss of DfID as a major bilateral malaria donor in Kenya will have a significant impact on program implementation, particularly in the strategic areas of vector control, case management, surveillance, monitoring and evaluation, and OR. Historically, the DfID malaria bilateral program contributed approximately $15–22 million per year to implementing the NMCP strategy. The DfID malaria program ended in March 2015; however, DfID granted a one-year, no-cost extension for programming to partners through March 2016.

The current Global Fund Round 10 malaria grant ends in December 2016. Kenya has been re-classified as a lower low-middle income country and will be required to meet a 20% threshold for counterpart financing. Additionally, it appears likely that the country allocation for malaria will decrease in the new funding model; Kenya was not eligible for incentive funding due to over-allocation in the Round 10 malaria grant.

The NMCP had the highest level of donor funding for program implementation in 2011 at approximately $100 million. From 2014–2016, the average total donor investment was $74 million per year. With the end of both DfID's bilateral malaria program and the Global Fund Round 10 malaria grant in 2016, the risk of inadequate financing for program implementation is extremely high. The estimated cost to implement the full NMCP strategy is $300 million per year; donor funding commitments beyond 2016 are currently unknown.

Although devolution to county government has led to uncertainties and disruptions, county government offers an opportunity to deliver health services directly to constituents and communities in a transparent and accountable manner. One of the basic tenets of devolution is to ensure resources and services are appropriately apportioned and delivered to communities. The overall malaria prevention and control program in Kenya could potentially benefit from devolution. For example, counties could harness additional government resources outside of the health system to deliver commodities (e.g., teachers and schools distributing ITNs) or engage the private-sector to invest in malaria prevention and control strategies that impact the work force and community (e.g., IRS in sugar-producing lake-endemic counties).

As county governments initiate planning and budgeting for health services delivery, advocacy and support for malaria prevention and control activities by partners and donors will be critical. PMI anticipates that additional resources will be required to initiate county malaria control programs over the transition period with the longer-term objective that counties will earmark resources to sustain and scale up malaria prevention and control interventions. In mid-2015, PMI met directly with four counties with the highest malaria burdens to advocate for political commitment and funding for the malaria control program and to leverage partnerships and investments by other key stakeholders to ensure the main malaria prevention and control strategies are implemented.

Over the last decade, there has been substantial political commitment at the national level for malaria prevention and control. PMI expects national level support to continue and that counties will prioritize malaria prevention and control interventions because of the significant impact malaria has on health service utilization and resources. With a limited number of health functions remaining at the national level, the NMCP, PMI and partners have an opportunity to focus on strengthening critical areas such as leadership development, policy, surveillance, monitoring and evaluation, and operational research.

III. OPERATIONAL PLAN

1. Insecticide-treated nets

NMCP/PMI objectives

The revised KMS objective is to attain universal coverage of ITNs, defined as reaching a ratio of one ITN for every two people, in conjunction with increasing use of those nets to 80% in all areas with a malaria risk by 2018. Universal coverage is to be achieved through multiple distribution channels. Thirty-six counties are defined by the NMCP to be endemic, epidemic-prone, or have seasonal malaria transmission and therefore, are targeted for routine ITN distribution to vulnerable populations, namely pregnant women and children less than one year of age, through ANC and EPI clinics. Twenty-three counties are targeted for regular free mass ITN distribution campaigns, which are conducted on a rolling basis every three years. Other channels for ITNs include social marketing through a private-sector partner, a pilot community distribution via CHVs, and commercial outlets.

PMI's objective is in line with the NMCP's objective to achieve universal coverage and increase use. Historically, PMI has supported routine distribution to vulnerable populations through ANC and EPI clinics (50% of total need) and mass ITN distribution campaigns. In 2014–2015, PMI supported a pilot community distribution channel utilizing CHVs.

Progress since PMI was launched

Since 2008, PMI has procured 13.8 million ITNs and distributed 7.4 million through two channels, health facilities and mass campaigns. Through June 2015, 6.9 million ITNs have been distributed free through routine ANC and EPI clinics in 36 counties to reach the most vulnerable populations, pregnant women and children under age one year. Another 2.6 million ITNs will be distributed through ANC and EPI channels from mid-2015 to mid-2017. In the 2011–2012 mass ITN distribution campaign, 500,000 ITNs were distributed in the coastal counties in the final phase. In the last half of 2015, 3.8 million ITNs will be distributed in 5 western Kenya counties as part of phase 4 of the 2014–2015 rolling universal coverage mass distribution campaign in 23 counties.

Despite substantial investments in ITNs by PMI and other partners for over a decade, only 59% of households have at least one ITN and just 34% have at least one ITN per two persons (i.e., universal coverage) as of 2014.[17] Access to ITNs at the household level appears to be the primary factor associated with use in both children under five years of age and pregnant women.[18]

Communication and promotion efforts to increase uptake and utilization of ITNs were focused initially on national mass media campaigns, particularly around universal coverage mass distributions. Between the mass distributions, PMI re-focused efforts on BCC and IPC at the community-level in high-burden areas where ITN usage has historically been low.

---

[17] Kenya National Bureau of Statistics (KNBS), Ministry of Health (MOH) [Kenya], and ICF International. 2015. Kenya Demographic and Health Survey Key Indicators 2014. Nairobi, Kenya: KNBS, MOH, and ICF International.
[18] Aloo, S. Findings of the 2014 malaria TRaC study among populations living in different malarial zones of Kenya. Presented at: National Malaria Control Program Monitoring and Evaluation Technical Working Group Meeting; 2014 December 3; Nairobi, Kenya.

Progress during the last 12–18 months

- Regular free mass ITN distribution: In 2014–2015, a rolling universal coverage mass distribution campaign is being conducted in at least four phases and will distribute at least 13.6 million ITNs in 23 counties. The first phase was financed by Global Fund and implemented by the NMCP and county/sub-county health management teams in September 2014 in five malaria-endemic counties (i.e., Migori, Homa Bay, Kisumu, Siaya, and Vihiga) in western Kenya. The first phase included the three counties (i.e., Migori, Homa Bay, and Kisumu) where IRS was last implemented in 2012. Almost 3 million ITNs were distributed in the first phase. Post-campaign administrative data demonstrated that a mean of 0.5 ITNs per person and 2.8 ITNs per household were distributed across the five counties.[19] An independent post-campaign coverage survey was not conducted.

  Phase two was funded and implemented by an international non-governmental organization (NGO) in West Pokot, an epidemic-prone county, in November 2014. Approximately 350,000 ITNs were distributed. Phases three and four are projected to take place in mid-to-late 2015. PMI is funding the procurement and distribution of 3.8 million ITNs in 5 counties; Global Fund is financing the procurement and distribution of 5.4 million ITNs for the remaining 12 counties. In late 2014, the NMCP added partial coverage of three counties with irrigation schemes to the mass distribution campaign; however, to date, no donor has been identified for the additional nets required.

- Routine distribution to vulnerable populations: Routine distribution is targeted to vulnerable populations living in malaria-endemic, epidemic-prone, and seasonal-transmission counties and goes beyond the geographic areas targeted in mass distribution campaigns. The NMCP supports routine distribution of free ITNs to pregnant women and children under one year of age through approximately 4,000 ANC and EPI clinics in 36 counties. The NMCP targets children less than one year of age primarily for operational reasons. Children under one year of age attend EPI clinics for immunizations; approximately 90% of infants in Kenya receive at least one vaccine and should receive an ITN during the first EPI clinic visit.[20] ITNs are also distributed to persons living with HIV/AIDS as part of the standard package of care provided through comprehensive care clinics.

  Routine distribution remains the primary channel for access to free ITNs between mass distribution campaigns with support by DfID and PMI. However, the number of households reached through existing channels is not sufficient to maintain universal coverage. Nationally, only 34% of households have reached universal coverage; in the 14 endemic counties, the range of universal coverage is 30–61%.[21] Consequently, Kenya is piloting a community-based continuous distribution channel to replace nets in targeted households using CHVs to help maintain high coverage levels, with the ultimate goal of reducing the need for mass distribution campaigns. Results from the community-based continuous distribution pilot and a cost-effectiveness study of current distribution channels are expected in late 2015 and late 2016, respectively.

---

[19] Malaria Control Unit (MCU), Ministry of Health (MoH) [Kenya]. Planning and Implementation of Phase 1 Mass LLIN Campaign 2014. Nairobi: MoH, November 2014.
[20] United Nations Children's Fund (UNICEF). *State of the World's Children 2015*. New York: UNICEF, 2015.
[21] Kenya National Bureau of Statistics (KNBS), Ministry of Health (MOH) [Kenya], and ICF International. 2015. *Kenya Demographic and Health Survey Key Indicators 2014*. Nairobi, Kenya: KNBS, MOH, and ICF International.

- Social marketing of ITNs: Through a private-sector partner, DfID has supported a social marketing program, which sells 600,000-800,000 ITNs per year through community-based organizations in targeted areas. The socially-marketed ITNs sell for between $0.50–$1.50 each and are sold primarily in rural areas in endemic and epidemic-prone counties. The NMCP estimates that demand for socially-marketed nets exceeds current supply levels; however, DfID is ending support for the bilateral malaria program in Kenya which includes socially-marketed ITNs in 2016.

Commodity gap analysis

Table 2. ITN Gap Analysis

Calendar Year	2015	2016	2017	2018
Total targeted population for continuous distribution[1]	34,890,430	35,644,615	36,398,800	37,168,944
Continuous Distribution Needs in 36 Counties[1]				
Channel #1: ANC	1,570,069	1,604,008	1,637,947	1,672,603
Channel #2: EPI	1,395,617	1,425,785	1,455,952	1,486,758
Channel #3: continuous-distribution channel(s)[2]			100,000	100,000
Estimated Total Need for Continuous	2,965,686	3,029,793	3,193,899	3,259,361
Mass Distribution Needs in 23 Full and 3 Partial Counties[2,3]				
2014–2015 mass campaign[3]	10,090,993			
2017–2018 mass campaign[4]			3,771,973	10,457,384
Estimated Total Need for Campaigns	10,090,993		3,771,973	10,457,384
Total Calculated Need: Routine and Campaign	**13,056,679**	**3,029,793**	**6,965,872**	**13,716,745**
Partner Contributions				
ITNs carried over from previous year				
ITNs from Global Fund Round 10, Phase 1 – campaign	5,500,212			
ITNs from Global Fund Round 10, Reprogramming[3] – campaign			3,771,973	2,858,027
ITNs from DFID – ANC/EPI channels	800,000			
ITNs planned with PMI funding	5,300,000	2,500,000	1,500,000	1,500,000
Total ITNs Available	**11,600,212**	**2,500,000**	**5,271,973**	**4,358,027**
Total ITN Surplus (Gap)	**(1,456,467)**	**(529,793)**	**(1,693,899)**	**(9,358,718)**

[1]Kenya Global Fund Malaria Round 10, Request for Renewal (Phase 2) Proposal (September 2013)
[Note: Quantification through 2017; extrapolation to 2018]
[2]Specific additional continuous distribution channel(s) will be identified during a 2016 review and planning exercise.
[3]Planning and Implementation of Phase 1 Mass LLIN Campaign: National Report (November 2014)
[Note: Revised quantification to fully cover 23 counties and 3 additional partial counties]
[4]Kenya Global Fund Malaria Round 10, Reprogramming Request (January 2015)

Plans and justification

With FY 2016 funds, the NMCP and PMI will focus efforts on maintaining a continuous supply of nets and a robust routine distribution system for ITNs as described above. PMI will support approximately 50% of the ITN need (i.e., 1.5 million nets) for the current routine distribution channel (i.e., ANC and EPI) to target the most vulnerable populations.

PMI will also support alternate approaches and continuous distribution channels in one county with both ITNs and implementation activities to maintain universal coverage following the 2017–2018 mass distribution campaign to address sustainability concerns. The specific approaches and channels targeted for PMI support will be based on the findings and recommendations from two ITN analyses that will be completed in 2016. First, PMI is supporting an economic evaluation of the five current ITN distribution channels that combines cost and coverage data to determine the most cost-effective channel(s) and inform future ITN policies and programs. Second, PMI is supporting an assessment of the scope of the current ITN continuous distribution channels and modeling of potential additional approaches/channels that are in the KMS 2014–2018 but not currently implemented. Following a review of these two analyses, PMI in coordination with the NCMP, counties, partners, stakeholders and donors, will determine whether implementing a pilot, proof-of-concept ITN program to maintain universal coverage in one county is warranted.

PMI will continue to support advocacy, communications, and social mobilization activities to inform ITN access and usage behaviors in hard-to-reach and general at-risk populations. The advocacy, communication, and social mobilization activities are described further in the Behavior Change Communication section.

Proposed activities with FY 2016 funding: (**$8,100,000**)

1. **Procure ITNs for routine distribution**: Provide approximately 50% (1.5 million) of the ITNs required for routine distribution. The ITNs will be distributed free-of-charge to pregnant women and children less than one year of age through over 4,000 ANC and EPI clinics as part of the routine distribution program. *($6,000,000)*

2. **Logistic and program support for routine ITN distribution**: Provide logistic support, including transportation and storage, for distribution of the estimated 1.5 million ITNs within the ANC and EPI clinic routine distribution system. *($1,500,000)*

3. **Procure ITNs for alternate continuous-distribution channel(s) in one endemic county:** Procure an additional 100,000 ITNs for alternate approaches and continuous distribution channels in one county to maintain universal coverage following the 2017–2018 mass distribution campaign. The initial total need in one county is estimated at one ITN per 1.8 persons or approximately 550,000 ITNs for an average-size county with a population of one million people. PMI is funding an initial 100,000 ITNs because the alternative continuous distribution project is anticipated to begin directly following the mass ITN campaign. *($400,000)*

4. **Logistic and program support for continuous ITN distribution:** Provide logistic and program support, including transportation and storage, for alternate approaches and continuous distribution channels in one county to maintain universal coverage following the 2017–2018 mass distribution campaign. The broad goal is to ensure universal coverage at the household level to improve ITN use, and the more specific goal is to quantify for counties and the NMCP

how many ITNs are required and at what time points using multiple channels in order to maintain universal coverage. *($200,000)*

5. **ITN durability monitoring:** Continue ITN durability field monitoring for a third year (Year 2 monitoring time point). Nets sampled, identified, and distributed in each of the four phases of the 2014–2015 mass campaign will have the following parameters measured in accordance with PMI guidance for this activity: attrition, durability, bioefficacy, and insecticide content analysis. The results of this activity will inform national and county ITN replacement policies, guidelines, and schedules. *(This activity is budgeted in the M&E section.)*

6. **Behavior change for correct and consistent use of ITNs:** Support and expand targeted advocacy, communication, and social mobilization activities to increase demand for, uptake, and usage of ITNs. Messages and mode of dissemination will be tailored to the venue and target group. Interpersonal communication (IPC) will be used in health facilities and ANC clinics for patients, in homes during visits by CHVs, and at *barazas* (i.e., community meetings) in villages and during public gatherings where health messages are delivered. Promoting correct and consistent use of ITNs will be a primary focus of this effort. *(This activity is budgeted in the BCC section.)*

2. Indoor residual spraying

NMCP/PMI objectives
The Kenya NMCP is developing a draft business plan for IRS (2015–2018) which is aligned with the Kenya Malaria Strategy (2014–2018), the Integrated Vector Management Strategy (draft) and the Insecticide Resistance Management Strategy (draft). The business plan calls for IRS targeted to endemic counties in western Kenya with the aim of achieving 80% spray coverage in targeted areas. The objective is to reduce malaria in the targeted areas while providing a buffer zone between endemic areas and highland, epidemic-prone areas of western Kenya. IRS would be done for three consecutive years and then moved to a new geographic area in western Kenya. Currently, the NMCP plans to provide coverage beginning in the south and expand north to other endemic districts bordering the highland epidemic-prone areas.

Progress since PMI was launched
PMI began spraying in Kenya in both highland and lowland districts (now sub-counties) in 2008. However, the NMCP shifted the IRS strategy to focus on lowland-endemic sub-counties beginning in 2010. In response, PMI shifted resources to target six sub-counties (i.e., parts of three counties) covering a total population of 2,435,836 in 2012. However, resistance to pyrethroids was observed in several locations in western Kenya and after the 2012 spray campaign, the NMCP decided to implement IRS with a carbamate insecticide. However, the insecticide was not registered for public health use in Kenya, and PMI and other donors stopped IRS until alternative insecticides could be registered for use in Kenya. There is now a single long-acting organophosphate that is registered for IRS use in Kenya. In 2016, the NMCP is planning for a small GoK-funded IRS program in a one sub-county in Migori County.

Table 3: PMI-supported IRS Activities 2008–2017

Calendar Year	Number of Counties Sprayed	Number of sub-Counties Sprayed	Insecticide Used	Number of Structures Sprayed§	Coverage Rate§	Population Protected§
2008	2	3	Lambda-cyhalothrin	764,050	96%	3,061,967
2009	2	3	Deltamethrin	517,051	94.6%	1,435,272
2010	2	5	Alpha-cypermethrin	503,707	97.1%	1,892,725
2011	2	5	Deltamethrin	485,043	89%	1,832,090
2012	3	6	Deltamethrin	460,447	98%	2,435,836
2013	0	0	NA	0	NA	0
2014	0	0	NA	0	NA	0
2015	0	0	NA	0	NA	0
2016*	1	1	Pirimiphos-methyl	85,000	NA	323,000
2017*	1	TBD	Pirimiphos-methyl	276,000	NA	1,400,000

* Represents projected targets based on national strategic plan and/or discussions with the NMCP.
§Figures presented through 2012 are from the Kenya IRS 2 Task Order Final Report.

Progress during the last 12–18 months

Direct support for IRS was suspended until Kenya revised their IVM strategy, developed a revised IRS business plan, and had registered non-pyrethroid insecticides for IRS. Furthermore, IRS funds were reprogrammed in 2014 to support the national ITN campaign which faced a 3.8 million net gap. However, entomological monitoring continued at 16 sites in western Kenya. Pyrethroid resistance has been observed in the major vectors, including *An. gambiae* s.s., *An. arabiensis* and *An. funestus* (Table 4). Additional data from other sources have confirmed the high levels of pyrethroid resistance in these species. In the past year, resistance to pyrethroids has been observed in all populations of *An. gambiae* s.l. including those near the lake where *An. arabiensis* predominates. *An. funestus*, which was reported to have largely disappeared after the scale-up of ITNs, has been reported to be increasing throughout western Kenya, often at higher numbers than *An. gambiae* or *An. arabiensis,* and has been demonstrated to be resistant to pyrethroid insecticides.[22] Over the past 12 months, routine entomological monitoring has confirmed that *An. funestus* is often the predominant mosquito at sentinel sites in western Kenya and is resistant to pyrethroid insecticides where numbers were available for testing.

---

[22] McCann RS, Ochomo E, Bayoh MN, Vulule JM, Hamel MJ, Gimnig JE, Hawley WA, Walker ED. 2014. Reemergence of Anopheles funestus as a vector of Plasmodium falciparum in western Kenya after long-term implementation of insecticide-treated bed nets. Am J Trop Med Hyg 90(4):597-604.

Table 4. Mortality of Mosquito Populations Exposed to Standard Papers in World Health Organization Resistance Assays—Kenya, 2014/2015

Insecticide Resistance Tests (% mortality)						
		Sub-County	Pyrethroid		Carbamate	Organo-phosphate
Species	County		Deltamethrin	Permethrin	Bendiocarb	Malathion
An. funestus	Homa Bay	Rachuonyo	24	---	---	---
An. funestus	Kisumu	Nyando	32	---	---	---
An. gambiae s.l.	Homa Bay	Rachuonyo	70	---	---	---
An. gambiae s.l.	Kisumu	Nyando	63	---	---	---
An. gambiae s.l.	Migori	Awendo	67	---	100	100
An. gambiae s.l.	Migori	Rongo	34	---	---	---
An. gambiae s.l.	Siaya	Gem	47	40	75	100
An. gambiae s.l.	Siaya	Siaya	48	46	88	100
An. gambiae s.l.	Siaya	Ugunja	39	43	---	100

Cells highlighted in gray indicate areas with confirmed resistance (mortality <90%).

Plans and justification

Despite the challenges, the NMCP and PMI remain committed to implementing IRS. Malaria in western Kenya remains persistently high despite relatively high coverage with ITNs and the increasing availability of AL. Recent modeling of malaria burden reduction in western Kenya suggests that IRS is needed to significantly reduce the burden of malaria in endemic counties.[23] Furthermore, data from a study in Bungoma County suggests that pyrethroid resistance may be on the verge of compromising the effectiveness of ITNs, suggesting the need for alternatives to pyrethroid insecticides is increasingly urgent.[24] Lastly, there is anecdotal evidence from other countries that IRS with non-pyrethroids may result in a reversal of pyrethroid resistance in malaria vectors. Thus, IRS with a non-pyrethroid insecticide might help maintain the effectiveness of ITNs. The NMCP is planning a small-scale IRS program in one sub-county of Migori County in 2016 using an organophosphate insecticide. Local county governments have also expressed interest in providing some support for IRS. PMI will work with the NMCP and local county governments to determine the most appropriate target area(s) for IRS beyond 2016. Currently, organophosphates are the only insecticide class which is registered in Kenya to which there is no known resistance. Therefore, PMI will support IRS with an organophosphate insecticide.

Given the high levels of resistance to pyrethroid insecticides, PMI plans to continue entomologic monitoring at sites in and around IRS program implementation in western Kenya. Mosquito densities will be monitored in and around the GoK and PMI IRS areas. Cone bioassays will be conducted to assess the quality of IRS applications while resistance monitoring will be conducted to determine the susceptibility of local mosquito populations. Resistance monitoring to date has relied on WHO resistance assays. Beginning in 2015–2016, intensity assays using the CDC bottle bioassay will be incorporated into selected entomological surveillance sites for comparison to the WHO resistance assays and to better quantify the degree of pyrethroid resistance.

---

[23] Malaria Control and Evaluation Partnership in Africa, unpublished data.
[24] Ochomo EO, Bayoh NM, Walker ED, Abongo BO, Ombok MO, Ouma C, Githeko AK, Vulule J, Yan G, Gimnig JE. 2013. The efficacy of long-lasting nets with declining physical integrity may be compromised in areas with high levels of pyrethroid resistance. Malar J. 12:368.

1. **IRS implementation and management:** Support IRS in one malaria endemic county in western Kenya, reaching an estimated 276,000 structures and protecting an estimated 1,400,000 people. *($7,000,000)*

2. **Entomologic monitoring:** Continue support for entomologic monitoring with routine surveys of vector density and insecticide-resistance monitoring of mosquitoes collected from sentinel surveillance sites in at least five counties, which includes any county or counties where PMI is conducting IRS. Resistance will be monitored through both WHO susceptibility test kits and intensity bioassays. Conduct entomological and insecticide resistance monitoring in areas identified by the NMCP as having gaps in data. *($320,000)*

3. **Supplies for entomologic monitoring:** Provide collection equipment, supplies for insecticide resistance testing and reagents for molecular identification of species and resistance markers. *($10,000)*

4. **Technical assistance—CDC:** Support two visits from CDC to provide technical assistance to the entomological monitoring program and specifically, IRS implementation activities. *($29,000)*

3. Malaria in pregnancy

NMCP/PMI objectives

The objective of the revised KMS 2014–2018 aims at ensuring that 80% of people living in malaria-risk areas are using appropriate malaria prevention interventions. In the case of malaria in pregnancy (MIP), a close working relationship with the Reproductive Maternal and Newborn Health (RMNH) Unit ensures that all pregnant women have access to the overall ANC package for maternal health which has three key malaria strategies namely, intermittent preventive treatment (IPTp), provision of ITNs, and prompt diagnosis and treatment of fever due to malaria.

Kenya adopted the WHO's updated policy on IPTp in 2012, and recently also adopted the 2013 consensus statement by broad MIP stakeholders, governments, multilaterals, bilaterals, and NGOs to optimize the delivery of MIP interventions. Intermittent preventive treatment with sulfadoxine-pyrimethamine (SP) is recommended only in the 14 counties (i.e., coastal and lake) with endemic malaria. Doses should be administered by directly observed therapy at each visit after quickening at four-week intervals to ensure all pregnant women receive a minimum of two doses. Women receive a free ITN at the first ANC visit and BCC messaging to encourage correct hanging of the net and consistent usage. As part of the current case management strategy by which all suspected malaria cases must be tested before treatment, all pregnant women are tested for malaria during antenatal care profiling and during subsequent visits for any signs or symptoms of malaria. The first-line treatment for uncomplicated malaria is oral quinine in the first trimester and AL in the second and third trimesters. The recommended treatment for severe malaria in pregnancy is parenteral artesunate. The national diagnosis and treatment guidelines recommend that pregnant women receive ferrous sulfate (200 mcg) and folic acid (0.4 mg) at all ANC visits and evaluation for anemia during the first and fourth ANC visits. If a woman is found to be anemic, diagnostic testing for malaria is recommended. Any women presenting to ANC with signs or symptoms of malaria should also be tested for malaria and if positive, treated in accordance with guidelines.

Progress since PMI was launched

Since PMI started supporting MIP interventions, a total of 840,000 doses of SP have been procured and more than 15,000 healthcare workers trained on the malaria in pregnancy package of interventions. PMI has also supported the Kenya Medical Supplies Agency (KEMSA) to redistribute 628,000 SP tablets to health facilities with shortages in nine malaria-endemic counties.

Despite Kenya having adopted the MIP strategy more than 16 years ago, IPTp coverage has remained below the national target of 80%. A gradual increase from 15 to 25% occurred between the MIS 2007 and 2010. In the recently released 2014 DHS, ANC coverage of pregnant women who make four or more visits rose to 58% from 47% in the 2008/9DHS. Late ANC attendance is still a challenge with only about 52% receiving care before the sixth month. While ANC visits provide an opportunity for administration of IPTp doses, additional community-based MIP activities began with PMI support in 2011. These activities include MIP messaging, use of community data collection tools to capture IPTp uptake, and early referral of pregnant women to health facilities to access ANC and IPTp services. CHVs do not administer IPTp, but refer pregnant women to ANC clinics for antenatal care, including IPTp.

Progress during the last 12–18 months

PMI has continued to support MIP activities at the national, county, facility and community levels. At the national level, PMI has supported the management and coordination of the MIP TWG meetings under the leadership of the RMNH department including keeping all stakeholders informed about MIP activities by distributing minutes of TWG meetings. At the county and sub-county levels, PMI has supported the development of county and sub-county MIP work plans (2014/5) in 5 of the 14 counties (Homa Bay, Migori, Kisumu, Bungoma, and Kakamega).

PMI supported RMNH and NMCP to train a team of four clinical mentor trainers (FP/RMNH). These mentors then trained a total of 44 new clinical mentors from the counties and sub-counties to orient health workers on the MIP guidelines. After the training, the 44 clinical mentors managed to orient 872 health workers in Bungoma and Kisumu Counties. In order to improve on IPTp data entry and management at health facilities, a team of 35 senior technical officers (including sub-county health records information officers, public health officers, Disease Surveillance and Response officers, and chief clinical officers) drawn from the five counties were trained on IPTp data management. The trained technical officers will carry out support supervision to assess the data entry processes in the health facilities.

At the community level, CHVs continued to follow up the previously registered 3,400 pregnant women in one sub-county of Bungoma. Of these women 3,094 (91%) received IPTp1, while 2074 (61%) received IPTp 2 and 1,462 (43%) received IPIp3. Bungoma County procured sulphdoxine-pyrimetahmine (SP) and distributed to all facilities after a quantification exercise supported by PMI. It is PMI's hope that other counties will borrow a leaf from Bungoma and procure SP for the counties. This example has already been shared with other county teams during their review meetings. The Government through KEMSA is in the process of procuring stocks of SP to replenish supplies in some facilities where the available supplies of SP expired in the month of April 2015.

Commodity gap analysis

The table reflects no gap at the central level in 2015 due to the SP that is being procured with FY 2015 funding by PMI and GOK funds. The orders are in process and supplies expected in-country between late 2015 and early 2016. Presently there are no stocks at KEMSA as remaining product expired in early

2015. The majority of the endemic counties did not factor procurement of SP into their budgets despite advice from the NMCP to include this, and their facilities are experiencing stockouts.

Table 5. SP Gap Analysis for Malaria in Pregnancy, Kenya, October 2015–September 2017

Calendar Year	2015	2016	2017
Total Population in Targeted Area	12,897,704	13,297,017	13,709,225
SP Needs			
Total number of pregnant women	580,374	598,366	616,915
Total SP Need (in treatments)**	**1,741,122**	**1,795,098**	**1,850,745**
Partner Contributions			
SP carried over/deficit from previous years	0	354,158	0
SP from MOH	435,280	0	0
SP from Global Fund	0	0	0
SP from Other Donors	0	0	0
SP planned with PMI funding	1,660,000	0	0
Total SP Available	2,095,280	0	0
Total SP Surplus (Gap)	354,158	(1,795,098)	(1,850,745)

Assumptions: population growth estimated at 3.1%. Average of 4.5% of the population would become pregnant in Coast, Western and Nyanza.
**One treatment is three tablets of SP.

Plans and justification
PMI will continue to support the implementation of MIP interventions, strengthening of ANC health worker capacity in endemic areas, dissemination of IPTp guidelines, and supportive supervision. In addition, leveraging on the large integrated health platform of the PEPFAR HIV/AIDS program, PMI will continue to support the community health strategy by building the capacity of CHVs on malaria in pregnancy interventions to mobilize, refer, track and report on pregnant women and ANC attendance in their communities. The combined approach of using CHVs, community health extension workers (CHEWs), and healthcare worker orientations through simplified guidelines and supportive supervision helps ensure that pregnant women attend ANC and receive IPTp and ITNs, in addition to other health services.

In the context of devolution, health service delivery activities are implemented at the county level. While PMI will continue to support MIP at the national level, FY 2016 funding will focus on continued step-wise scale up of the MIP package of interventions, including IPTp delivery and quality improvement frameworks, in health facilities in two new target endemic counties of Kisumu and Migori.

In addition, FY 2016 funding will support continued scale up of CHV training and supervision in the five counties of Bungoma, Homa Bay, Migori, Kakamega and Kisumu.

Due to the current challenge of stockouts of SP, PMI is proposing to reprogram some FY 2015 funds to procure approximately 1.7 million treatments of SP to fill the gap before the Government's supplies of SP are distributed to health facilities. However, PMI will not buy any SP with FY 2016 funding since the government has already issued a memo to all counties asking them to procure SP in the future. PMI will work with the NMCP, counties and other donors to ensure SP commodity needs are met.

Proposed activities with FY 2016 funding: ($800,000)

1. **Sensitize and train healthcare workers in facilities on malaria prevention and management strategies for pregnant women:** Healthcare workers in all healthcare facilities that provide ANC services in the five counties will be trained, with an estimated target of over 800 healthcare facilities. Activities will include the orientation and training of facility in-charges and health service providers on the MIP package and ANC data collection, and implementation of a quality improvement framework for healthcare facilities providing ANC services. *($350,000)*

2. **Sensitize, orient, and supervise CHVs:** This activity will include the orientation, training and supervision of CHVs to increase early referral to ANC services, register all pregnancies for follow-up, and provide case management and ITNs. CHVs are trained to undertake BCC activities and to refer and follow pregnant women to ensure that they receive IPTp at health facilities. An estimated 5,500 CHVs will be sensitized and oriented using the community strategy and other innovative approaches. The target is to reach approximately 50,000 women of reproductive age with community MIP messages and services in five counties. *($350,000)*

3. **Strengthen national and county policy and monitoring capacity:** Though most of the activity implementation will be at county level, limited support will be provided at the national level in the areas of policy and monitoring and evaluation of MIP-specific activities. Technical assistance support will be provided to counties on MIP, as necessary. *($100,000)*

4. **Case management**

   a. **Diagnosis and Treatment**

NMCP/PMI objectives
The *National Guidelines for the Diagnosis, Treatment and Prevention of Malaria in Kenya* (2014) state that patients with symptoms of malaria (i.e., fever) in all age groups and all epidemiologic settings should be tested by either microscopy or RDT, and only those who test positive should be given antimalarial treatment. However, appropriate treatment should not be denied or delayed due to a lack of available testing. The national case management guidelines do not provide clarity on which diagnostic method is most appropriate at the different levels of the health system. Microscopy is being used where it exists, including some lower-level health facilities despite quality concerns. Kenya recommends AL as the first-line treatment for uncomplicated malaria and parenteral artesunate for severe malaria. Quinine is still used in health facilities because its less expensive, stock is readily available from previous KEMSA procurements, and artesunate is not fully rolled out. Historically, PMI has procured and distributed RDTs and AL to all public health facilities; since 2014, distribution has extended to the community level via linked health facilities in malaria endemic counties.

Progress since PMI was launched

The NMCP, PMI, and partners have invested in three key areas related to malaria diagnostics: 1) procurement and distribution of diagnostic commodities; 2) training of clinical and laboratory personnel in the use of these diagnostic tools; and 3) implementation of QA/QC systems for malaria microscopy and RDTs. Since 2008, PMI has procured and distributed over 160 microscopes and almost 12.6 million RDTs and supported strengthening of diagnostics by training over 4,700 healthcare workers. PMI has also procured almost 48.7 million AL treatments and has trained over 5,000 healthcare workers on national case management guidelines.

The establishment of a QA/QC system for malaria diagnostics as described in the national malaria laboratory guidelines was initially operationalized in late 2012 with support from PMI, DfID, WHO, and World Bank. The initial focus was two-fold: (1) to train a cadre of QA officers from an experienced pool of laboratory technicians at county and sub-county hospitals and public health laboratories, and (2) to develop standard operating procedures, tools and supervisory checklists for both internal and external QA/QC at the health-facility level. With initial funding for supportive supervision and laboratory strengthening from Global Fund and PMI and technical assistance from WHO, the counties are being encouraged by the NMCP and partners to incorporate routine QA/QC systems for laboratory diagnostics, including malaria, into their county health plans and budgets. Malaria diagnostic services have also benefited from integrated laboratory supervision and QA/QC systems funded primarily by PEPFAR.

Progress during the last 12–18 months
In 2014, PMI procured over 6.5 million RDTs and delivered almost 3.3 million to the national level. The biannual Quality of Care (QoC) survey—which includes standard PMI end-use verification questions—measures diagnostic test and medicine availability in Kenya, among other indictors. Data from both routine supply chain monitoring and the QoC survey conducted in September 2014 indicated substantial progress in the availability of RDTs nationally (Figures 4 and 5). The 2014 DHS reported that 35% of children with fever in the last two weeks had blood taken for testing, which is an increase from 12% in the MIS 2010.[25,26] The increase is primarily the result of an improved RDT supply because the availability of microscopy has been stable across surveys at approximately 50% (Figure 5). Testing of patients with fever and suspected malaria increased from 24% at baseline in 2010 to 62% by September 2014.[27] In early 2015, PMI supported an assessment of diagnostic capacity and clinical case management practices at health-facility level in the high-burden, malaria-endemic counties to prioritize and focus diagnostic and case management strengthening activities. Kenya has insufficient human and financial resources to scale up the QA/QC plan for malaria diagnostics to the more than 5,000 public health facilities in the country. However, with the transition to county health service delivery, there is an opportunity to integrate supportive supervision of malaria microscopy and RDTs into broader laboratory supervision and quality assurance platforms.

[25] Kenya National Bureau of Statistics (KNBS), Ministry of Health (MOH) [Kenya], and ICF International. 2015. *Kenya Demographic and Health Survey Key Indicators 2014.* Nairobi, Kenya: KNBS, MOH, and ICF International.
[26] Division of Malaria Control (DOMC) [Ministry of Public Health and Sanitation], Kenya National Bureau of Statistics (KNBS), and ICF Macro. *2010 Kenya Malaria Indicator Survey.* Nairobi: DOMC, KNBS and ICF Macro, 2011.
[27] Machini B, Nyandigisi A, Kigen S, Memusi D, Kimbui R, Mulinga J, Zurovac D, Kiptui R, Waqo E. Monitoring outpatient malaria case management under the 2010 diagnostic and treatment policy in Kenya-Progress 2010-2014. Malaria Control Program, Ministry of Health, November 2014.

Figure 4. Supply of Malaria Rapid Diagnostic Tests in Months at National Level—Kenya, January 2013–March 2015

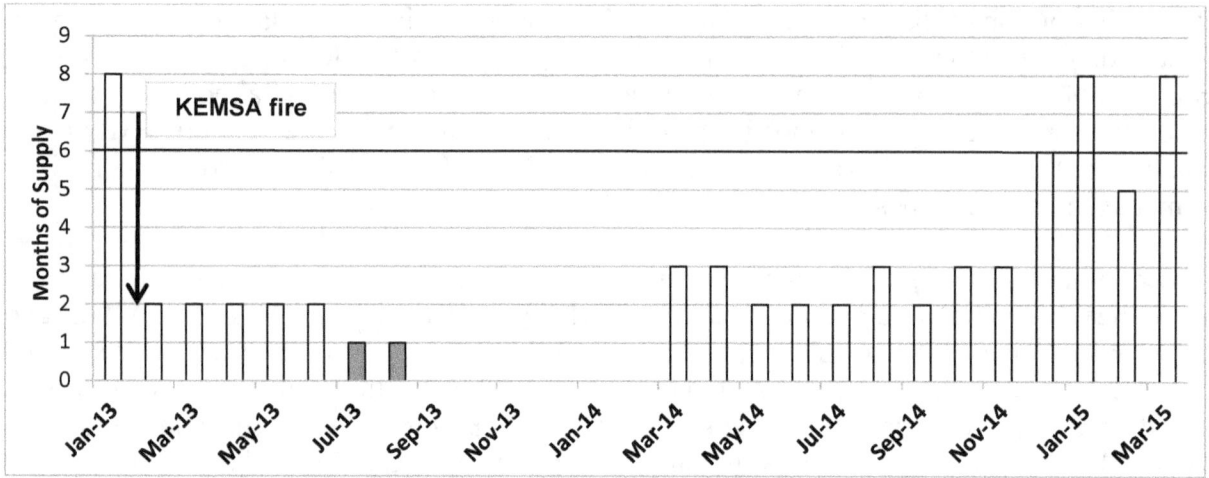

Notes: KEMSA=Kenya Medical Supply Agency; 6-month bar represents the minimum recommended supply level.

Figure 5: National trends in the coverage of health facilities with malaria diagnostics—Kenya, 2010–2014

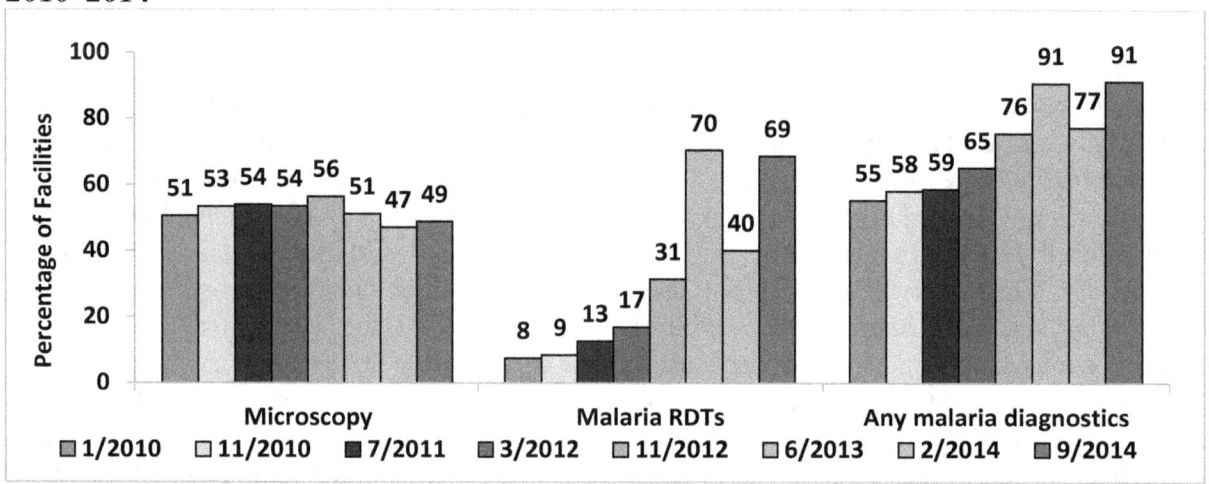

Notes: RDTs=rapid diagnostic tests
Reference: Machini B, Nyandigisi A, Kigen S, Memusi D, Kimbui R, Mulinga J, Zurovac D, Kiptui R, Waqo E. *Monitoring outpatient malaria case management under the 2010 diagnostic and treatment policy in Kenya-Progress 2010-2014*. Malaria Control Program, Ministry of Health, November 2014.

In 2014, PMI procured over 4 million AL treatments and delivered over 10.4 million AL treatments, which contributed to national AL stocks and complemented Global Fund procurement cycles. PMI also continued to strengthen the in-country supply chain system with the goal of an uninterrupted supply of AL to all public health facilities. Figure 6 shows AL stocks available at the national level from January 2013 through March 2015. National level stockouts of AL started in 2014 during the transition from a traditional, central medical store push system to a business-model pull system based on county orders and financing. Because of a history of chronic undersupply of commodities and limited capacity for quantification and forecasting by most counties, counties over-ordered AL, which caused stockouts at the national level in 2014. Prior to this transition, Kenya had not experienced a stockout at the central level for more than three years. At the health-facility level, the QoC survey data from September 2014 shows that health facilities started experiencing a reduction of AL availability during the transition to devolved health service delivery in late 2013 to early 2014 (Figure 7). Only 23% of facilities had all AL weight bands in stock on the day of the survey; 76% of facilities had at least one AL weight band in stock. The NMCP and partners, including PMI, have supported counties to improve quantification and forecasting of commodity needs based on routine DHIS2 data to ensure rational procurements.

Figure 6. Supply of Artemether-lumefantrine in Months at National Level—Kenya, January 2013–March 2015

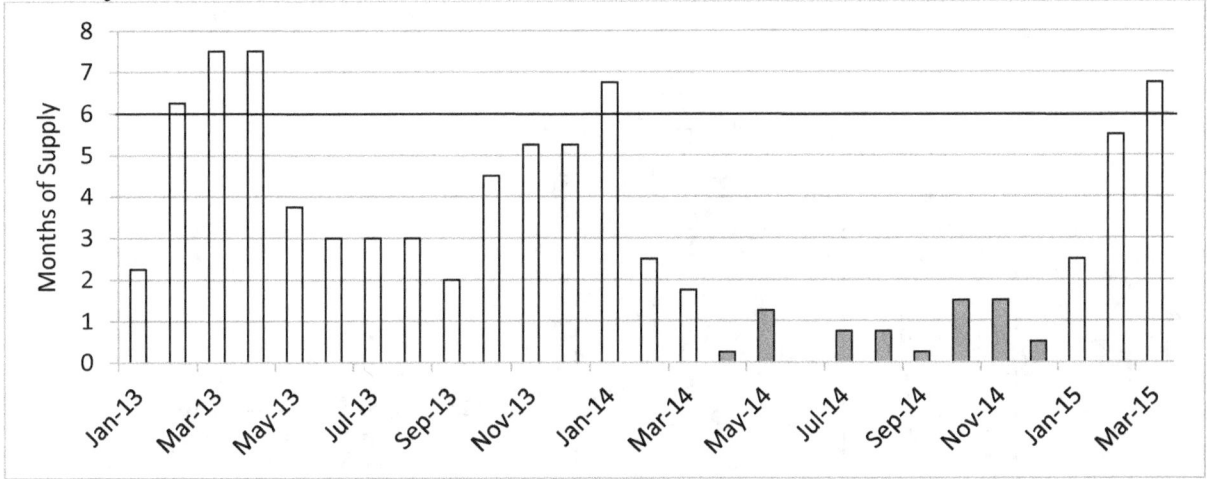

Notes: 6-month bar represents the minimum recommended supply level.

Figure 7: National trends in the availability of artemether-lumefantrine at health facilities on survey day—Kenya, 2010–2014

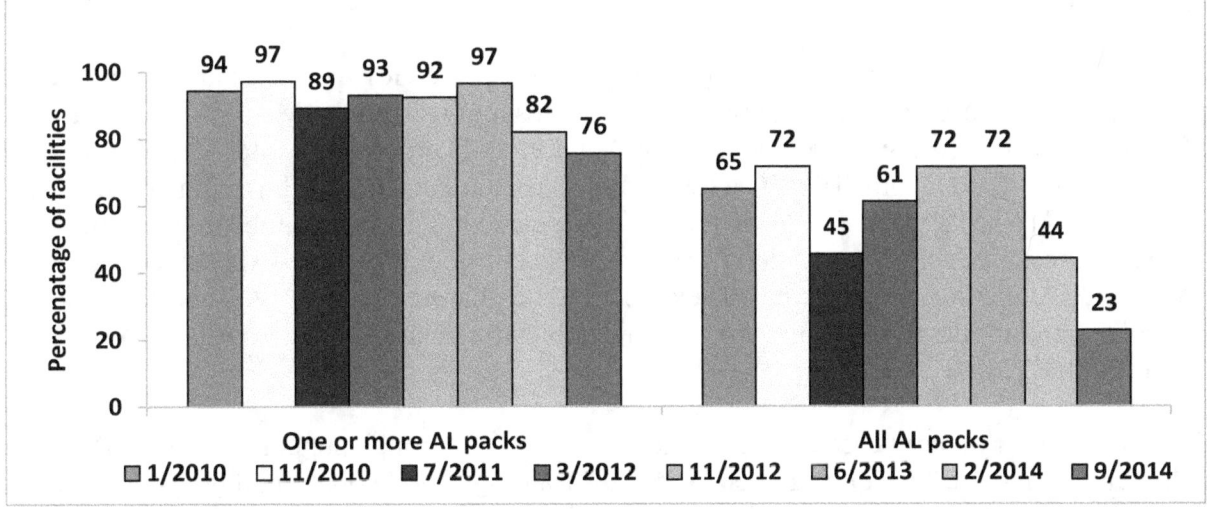

Notes: AL=artemether-lumefantrine
Reference: Machini B, Nyandigisi A, Kigen S, Memusi D, Kimbui R, Mulinga J, Zurovac D, Kiptui R, Waqo E. *Monitoring outpatient malaria case management under the 2010 diagnostic and treatment policy in Kenya-Progress 2010-2014*. Malaria Control Program, Ministry of Health, November 2014.

Nearly all malaria test-positive patients now receive appropriate drug treatment when available, although availability of AL to treat test-positive patients is lacking in some facilities. As measured by QoC surveys, in health facilities where both malaria diagnostics and AL were available, the percentage of test-positive patients treated with AL has remained relatively consistent and near 90% (Figure 8). The percentage of patients who received a malaria medicine despite testing negative for malaria continued to decline from a baseline of over half (53%) of all patients to just 10% in September 2014 (Figure 8). However, even when malaria diagnostics are available, one-third of patients are not tested in accordance with the national case management guidelines (Figure 8). PMI supported refresher training of over 1,000 healthcare workers on malaria case management including RDT use in malaria-endemic counties in 2014.

Figure 8: National trends in health workers diagnostic and treatment adherence to national case management guidelines where malaria diagnostic services were available and AL was in stock—Kenya, 2010–2014

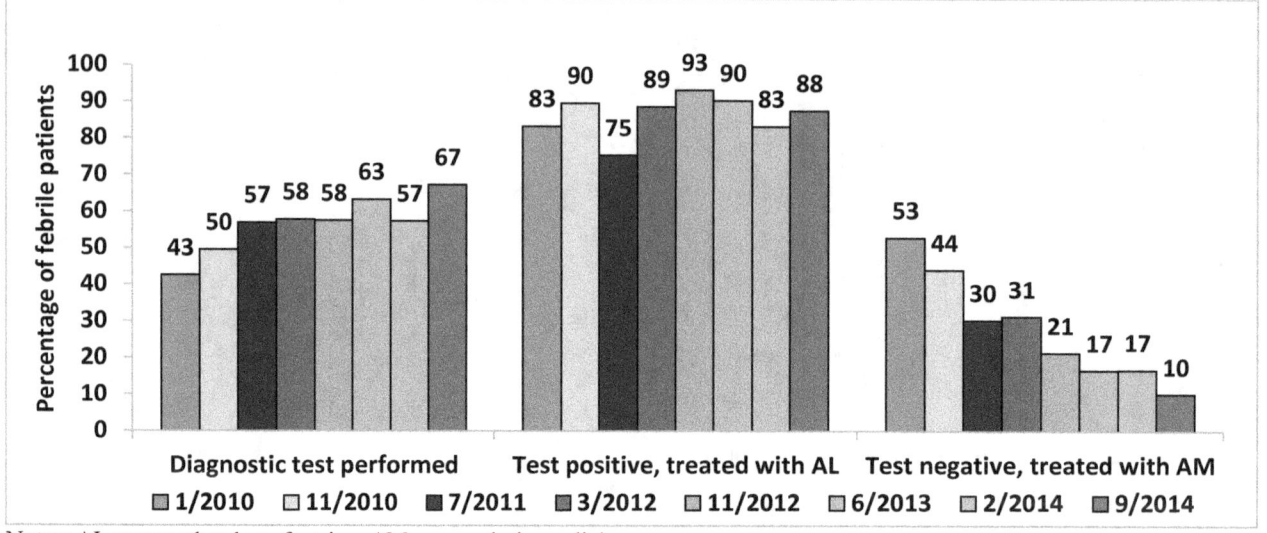

Notes: AL=artemether-lumefantrine, AM=any malaria medicine
Reference: Machini B, Nyandigisi A, Kigen S, Memusi D, Kimbui R, Mulinga J, Zurovac D, Kiptui R, Waqo E. *Monitoring outpatient malaria case management under the 2010 diagnostic and treatment policy in Kenya-Progress 2010-2014*. Malaria Control Program, Ministry of Health, November 2014.

In 2012, following the change in treatment policy for severe malaria, the GoK procured and distributed 700,000 vials of injectable artesunate. In 2015, the NMCP, with support from the Medicines for Malaria Venture (MMV), Clinton Health Access Initiative (CHAI) and PMI, is procuring a total of 1.5 million vials (PMI 500,000, GoK 80,000, and CHAI 928,280) of injectable artesunate for the treatment of severe malaria leaving a gap of 119,518 vials. The NMCP has also trained over 14,000 healthcare workers on the use of parenteral artesunate for severe malaria. Artesunate is considerably more expensive than quinine, and MMV/CHAI support for artesunate is expected to be phased out by 2017. Therefore, the NMCP has prioritized procurement and distribution of injectable artesunate alongside AL for case management starting in FY2016.

Training and supervision for malaria case management was advanced through support for the CHV strategy, which includes malaria case management and RDT training. The Global Fund grant to AMREF has provided support for the training of over 7,700 CHVs and CHEWs and support for over 700 community units, which includes over 35,000 CHVs and 1,400 CHEWs providing services to a beneficiary population of 3.5 million people across 10 counties. Other partners have also provided training and support; PMI supported the training and supportive supervision of over 400 CHVs in the past year. The NMCP, AMREF, and PMI were able to take advantage of significant PEPFAR resources for improving the quality of health service delivery from the community to county levels through integrative programs; malaria-specific support is provided through implementing partners to communities, health facilities and sub-counties in the targeted 10 counties. With malaria community case management training and increased knowledge among CHVs, CHEWs, and healthcare providers, community units are now prioritizing malaria prevention messaging and interventions and initiating implementation of the malaria community case management strategy.

Malaria diagnostic services have benefited from integrated laboratory supervision and QA/QC systems funded primarily by PEPFAR. Health facilities providing malaria diagnostic services that had at least one quality control visit in the three months prior to the latest QoC survey increased from 9% at baseline in 2010 to 41% by 2014.[28] However, supervision for malaria RDTs was only 15%. Case management has also benefited from integrated clinical supervision with support from PEPFAR, Global Fund, PMI, and other partners. In the three months preceding the September 2014 QoC survey, 65% of health facilities had received at least one supervisory visit, and 31% had received at least one visit that included a malaria case management topic.

Although PMI has not invested in private-sector case management activities in Kenya, DfID and CHAI have provided funding and implemented projects aimed at increasing RDT use in the private sector and changing national policy to allow point-of-service testing at registered pharmacies. Pilot projects are ongoing in the coastal counties of Kilifi, Kwale, and Mombasa with the objective to increase access to RDTs in the private sector. In addition, when the Affordable Medicines Facility – malaria (AMFm) ended in Kenya in 2013, DfID funded an extension of AMFm to increase the affordability and accessibility of ACTs in the private sector. An MIP case management study conducted by a malaria FELTP resident and supported by PMI found that by October 2013, 91% of rural, informal drug outlets stocked quality-assured AL and at the price target of $1.00 per treatment course but only 10% of drug outlets stocked RDTs[29]. Kenya has a large and robust private health sector, including a growing health insurance component, with numerous commercial, governmental and non-governmental partners working on quality of care initiatives from diagnostic algorithms to physician detailing to pay-for-performance incentives.

---

[28] Machini B, Nyandigisi A, Kigen S, Memusi D, Kimbui R, Mulinga J, Zurovac D, Kiptui R, Waqo E. Monitoring outpatient malaria case management under the 2010 diagnostic and treatment policy in Kenya-Progress 2010-2014. Malaria Control Program, Ministry of Health, November 2014.

[29] Kioko U, Riley C, Dellicour S, et al. The availability and cost of malaria medications and rapid diagnostic tests in drug outlets in rural Siaya County, western Kenya. Poster (#241) presented at the American Society of Tropical Medicine and Hygiene 63rd Annual Meeting, New Orleans, LA, 2–6 November 2014.

Commodity gap analysis

Table 6: RDT Gap Analysis

Calendar Year	2015	2016	2017
RDT Needs			
Target population at risk for malaria	46,036,194	47,349,209	48,699,776
Total number projected fever cases seeking care (all sectors)	43,734,384	44,981,749	46,264,787
Total projected number of fever cases public sector (facilities)	29,870,584	30,722,534	31,598,850
Percent of fever cases confirmed with microscopy	30%	30%	30%
Percent of fever cases confirmed with RDT	70%	70%	70%
Total projected number of fever cases public sector facilities tested with an RDT	**20,909,409**	**21,505,774**	**22,119,195**
Total RDTs needed for public sector community case management	**2,011,782**	**2,069,160**	**2,128,180**
Total RDT Needs	**22,921,191**	**23,574,934**	**24,247,375**
Partner Contributions			
RDTs carried over from previous year	*0*	*0*	*5,479,194*
RDTs from Global Fund	16,308,583	17,754,128	5,029,038
RDTs planned with PMI funding	3,750,000	11,300,000	8,000,000
Total RDTs Available	20,058,853	29,054,128	18,508,232
Total RDT Surplus (Gap)	-2,862,608	5,479,194	-5,739,144
Assumption: 95% of the population will experience a fever and seek care. Of those seeking care for fever, 68.3% are in the public sector and 4.6% are in the community (KMIS 2010).			

Table 7: ACT Gap Analysis

Calendar Year	2015	2016	2017
ACT Needs			
Target population at risk for malaria	46,036,194	47,349,209	48,699,776
Total number projected fever cases seeking care (all sectors)[a]	43,734,384	44,981,749	46,264,787
Total projected number of fever cases public sector (facilities)[a]	29,870,584	30,722,534	31,598,850
Total projected number of fever cases community level[a]	2,011,782	2,069,160	2,128,180
Total projected fever cases public sector facilities and community level	31,882,366	32,791,694	33,727,030
Total projected number of malaria cases public sector facility and community[b]	15,941,183	14,756,263	13,490,812
Factoring in additional ACT needs due to lack of compliance to negative test results[c]	17,375,889	15,494,076	13,490,812
Total Adjusted ACT Needs	17,375,889	15,494,076	13,490,812
Partner Contributions			
ACTs carried over from previous year	*0*	*2,084,417*	*0*
ACTs from Global Fund	5,717,066	6,110,201	5,476,188
ACTs planned with PMI funding	13,743,240	6,950,000	4,500,000
Total ACTs Available	19,460,306	15,144,618	9,976,188
Total ACT Surplus (Gap)	2,084,417	-349,458	-3,514,624

[a] 95% of the population will experience a fever and seek care. Of those seeking care for fever, 68.3% are in the public sector and 4.6% are in the community (KMIS 2010).
[b] Number of malaria cases is expected to be 50% of all fever cases tested based on the Test Positivity Rate (TPR) in the malaria surveillance bulletin issue 8. The TPR is projected to decline 5% per year due to vector control and expanding diagnostics.
[c] Total need is adjusted for adherence to negative test results (QoC round 8 report, 91% compliance) at 91%, 95%, and 100% in 2015, 2016 and 2017, and assumes 100% testing.

Plans and justification

In FY 2016, PMI will build on the progress to date in scaling-up malaria diagnostic testing and QA/QC systems and case management strengthening. PMI supports biannual national quantification analyses to ensure that RDT and AL requirements are properly forecasted. The projected annual RDT need has increased as the country target for diagnostic coverage has increased. PMI will procure approximately 8 million RDTs to help meet the projected national RDT need based on testing of all suspected malaria and meeting 100% of country need. The national AL need has been decreasing due to prevention efforts, increased availability of diagnostics, and implementation of the "test, treat, track" policy. PMI will procure approximately 4.5 million AL treatments to help meet the projected national AL need. In addition in FY 2016, PMI will procure 500,000 vials of injectable artesunate to treat severe malaria as funding from MMV/CHAI will end in 2017.

PMI will support integrated strengthening of case management (i.e., strengthening diagnostic capacity and clinical case management proficiency together) at the health-facility, sub-county and county levels. Counties will be prioritized for support and case management activities will be based on the results of a case management assessment completed in mid-2015; with FY 2016 funding, over 800 public health facilities in the eight high-burden, high-priority counties in western Kenya will receive integrated case management support.

*Proposed activities with FY 2016 funding: **($9,993,000)***

1. **Procure RDTs:** Procure approximately 8 million RDTs, which represent ~30% of the total public sector facility and community need. *($2,560,000)*

2. **Procure AL:** Procure approximately 4.5 million AL treatments, which represent ~30% of the total public sector facility and community need. *($4,571,600)*

3. **Procure parenteral artesunate:** Procure approximately 500,000 vials of injectable artesunate for severe malaria, which represent ~30% of the total public sector need. *($1,300,000)*

4. **Logistic and program support for RDT, AL and parenteral artesunate distribution:** Provide warehousing, storage and distribution for RDTs, AL, and severe malaria medicines from central to facility level nationwide via KEMSA. *($841,400)*

5. **Capacity building for and strengthening of malaria diagnostics:** Support the appropriate and rational use of RDTs and microscopy at high-volume and community-linked health facilities in all eight malaria-endemic counties in western Kenya; the target for activity implementation is over 800 public health facilities. Activities will be integrated to strengthen all aspects of case management; the diagnostic component will include strengthening diagnostic capacity of existing laboratory and healthcare staff through refresher trainings and capacity building for supportive supervision, on-the-job training, and mentoring of county/sub-county/health-facility staff to enable case management improvements at the health-facility level. Support will also be provided for integrated implementation and strengthening of the QA/QC framework for malaria diagnostics in focus counties. *($400,000)*

6. **Capacity building for and strengthening of case management:** Support the appropriate and rational use of AL and parenteral artesunate at referral, high-volume and community-linked health facilities in all eight malaria-endemic counties in western Kenya; the target for activity implementation is over 800 public health facilities. Activities will be integrated to strengthen all aspects of case management in coordination; the clinical component will include strengthening clinical capacity of existing healthcare staff through refresher trainings and capacity building for supportive supervision, on-the-job training, and mentoring of county/sub-county/health-facility staff to improve the management of uncomplicated and severe malaria and malaria in pregnancy in line with national case management guidelines. *($300,000)*

7. **Technical assistance:** Support one CDC in-country visit to provide technical assistance for malaria diagnostics. *($10,000)*

8. **Technical assistance:** Support one CDC in-country visit to provide technical assistance for clinical malaria case management. *($10,000)*

b. Pharmaceutical Management

NMCP/PMI objectives
In line with the revised KMS 2014–2018, PMI has supported supply chain management activities at central, health-facility and community levels to ensure all MoH facilities have RDTs and all weight-based packs of AL, thereby preventing stockouts of essential malaria commodities.

Progress since PMI was launched
Since 2008, PMI has supported strengthening of supply chain management systems to ensure that over 12.5 million RDTs and 48.7 million AL doses procured were distributed to beneficiaries. Although, strengthening of the supply chain has largely improved the availability of RDTs and AL at the central and health facility levels countrywide and the community level in high burden counties, stock outs were experienced in 2014. These stock outs were due to the Railway Development Levy (RDL) that was introduced by the government causing substantial delays in importation and clearance of donor funded program commodities. The Government of Kenya has since waived RDL costs for all donor-procured commodities across disease programs.

Since 2010 PMI has also provided support to the NMCP, Pharmacy and Poisons Board (PPB) and National Quality Control Laboratory (NQCL) for quality monitoring of antimalarial medicines using Minilab® (i.e., a mobile mini-laboratory for rapid drug quality verification and counterfeit medicine detection supplied by Global Pharma Health Fund). To date, more than 30 staff from NMCP, PPB and NQCL have been trained, on the use of mini lab basic tests, sampling strategies and reporting for antimalarial medicines quality monitoring at 11 sentinel sites including two port of entry sites where in-flow of commodities is greatest and where counties with large populations and high malaria burden are situated have been established. PMI has also supported five rounds of Medicines Quality Monitoring (MQM). Since 2009, the number of medicines that have failed quality testing has declined dramatically.

Progress during the last 12–18 months
PMI supported the NMCP to strengthen commodity management at the national, county, and sub-county levels to ensure logistics data was available to inform forecasting, quantification, pipeline monitoring and procurement planning (Figures 4 and 6 in Diagnosis and Treatment sections) to prevent stockouts of malaria commodities at national and peripheral levels. The FY 2014/ 2015 National Annual Quantification for malaria commodities was undertaken in July 2014 and a midyear review conducted in January 2015. The 2015 review informed the malaria program on the current country stock situation, the anticipated gaps and provided an opportunity for the revision of delivery schedules of ACTs and RDTs that were still on order.

At the national level, PMI supported pipeline monitoring activities including the monthly malaria commodities stock status report which provides a snapshot of the current national malaria commodity stock levels, expected deliveries, and anticipated stockout periods. This report provided critical information that informed PMI procurements of 6 million ACTs and 3.4 million RDTs in July 2014 and an additional 300,000 ACTs in September 2014. PMI has continued to support the Drug Management Subcommittee (DMSC), a subcommittee of the Case Management Technical Working Group which meets monthly to discuss and address malaria commodity security issues. A key commodity security issue that the DMSC had to manage following the introduction of the pull system of distribution for counties was the irrational ordering of ACTs by facilities. To mitigate against stockouts caused by irrational ordering, the DMSC in October 2014 introduced the 'smart' push system for distribution of malaria commodities. This approach sets a limit on the maximum quantity of malaria medicines that can be supplied to a facility and is dependent on the level of care and epidemiological zone. Public health facilities began receiving malaria commodities through the smart push system of distribution in

December 2014. In 2015, PMI is supporting the NMCP to scale up use of artesunate for severe malaria treatment by procuring 500,000 vials of injectable artesunate which is expected to meet 31% of the annual national need. PMI is also procuring 1.7 million treatments of SP to fill the IPTp commodity gap in 14 malaria endemic counties.

At county level, building on its initial support to pharmacists and health management teams for commodity management training and orientation, PMI has continued to provide intensive support for routine malaria commodity reporting through the malaria commodity form in DHIS2 and capacity building to 15 priority county commodity security teams that have been formed to undertake quantification and track stock status for malaria commodities. In August 2014, PMI supported a meeting of county pharmacists to review the reporting performance on malaria indicators and to plan for inter- and intra-county redistribution of malaria commodities. The redistribution of malaria commodities from low transmission to endemic and epidemic prone counties was planned out by county pharmacists working collaboratively with county malaria coordinators in November 2014. Redistribution, though a resource intensive activity, is critical for preventing stockouts and reducing expiries. It is expected that once counties have improved their capacity for quantification, stock management, and use of data for decision making, stock redistribution will cease to be a priority.

PMI continues to support routine malaria commodity data reporting by health facilities through DHIS2. Although, the national health facilities reporting has remained above 60% in the period between mid-2014 and early 2015, the fifteen PMI-supported malaria endemic and epidemic counties have recorded consistently higher reporting rates averaging 88% over the same period (Figure 9).

Figure 9: Comparison of reporting rates for malaria commodities between high burden malaria priority counties and nationally

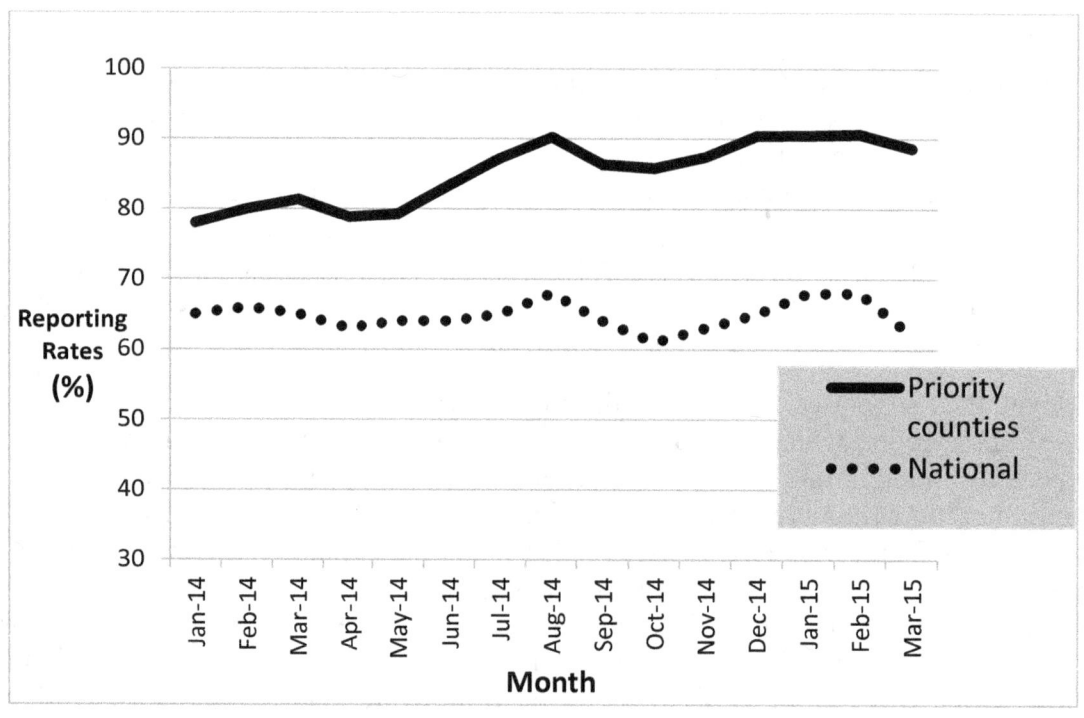

PMI continued to provide support to the NQCL for MQM. During the fifth round conducted in 2014, more than 800 samples were collected from 11 sites and tested using Minilab®. Thirty-eight failed samples were submitted to the Mission for Essential Drugs (MEDS) for QC testing and 20% of passed samples were sent to the NQCL for compendial testing. Five regulatory actions were taken on the failed samples which entailed seizure of medicines and criminal prosecution

As part of strengthening quality control of medicines in Kenya, since 2012 PMI has supported NQCL to pursue ISO 17025 accreditation. NQCL achieved this significant milestone and earned ISO 17025 accreditation in April 2015. This certification puts NQCL at the same standard with other internationally-recognized laboratories for medicines (tablets and suspensions) quality monitoring and testing. PMI is supporting PPB to establish a QC laboratory by providing technical assistance for concept and schematic design of the PPB lab to meet international standards and providing a road map for the required lab equipment and training needs.

Significant challenges remain in ensuring rational ordering – based on actual need and a continuous supply of malaria commodities to the health-facility and community levels in the context of devolution to 47 counties. A shortage of manual malaria reporting tools in the counties has also been noted as contributing to lower reporting rates for malaria commodities.

Plans and justification
PMI will continue to provide support at the national level for strengthening of policy and structures for supply chain management as well as strategic and operational planning for the 47 counties to ensure a continuous and uninterrupted availability of malaria commodities. In priority high burden malaria counties PMI will continue to provide intense support to build capacity for forecasting, quantification, reporting, and stock management of malaria commodities within county teams. PMI will also support the FY2015/16 annual quantification exercise expected to be conducted in June 2015 and the projected ACT and RDT estimated country need in MOP 2016 and based on the FY2014/15 quantification report will be updated to reflect the revised estimates.

PMI will also continue to support financial requirements for warehousing and distribution of malaria commodities from central to health facility levels and for inter- and intra-county re-distribution of commodities during the devolution transitional period to prevent health-facility level stock outs and to expand availability of commodities at community level.

Proposed activities with FY 2016 funding: (*$1,300,000*)

1. **Strengthen supply chain management for malaria commodities at the national level:** PMI will continue to provide support to the NMCP and KEMSA to strengthen supply chain management and build capacity to ensure commodity data is available and used to accurately forecast and quantify commodity needs, monitor the commodity pipeline and plan procurements to mitigate delays in Global Fund cycles and prevent stockouts at all levels of the health system. Areas of technical and operational support to the NMCP will include: a systematic approach for transitioning back to the pull system from the smart push system, support to malaria endemic counties implementing community case management for malaria to ensure they receive both RDTs and AL to enable them implement the "test, treat and track" policy at the community level. Support to KEMSA will include strengthening distribution of malaria commodities, monitoring and evaluation of performance with emphasis on on-time order delivery performance. PMI will continue to support end-use verification surveys (budgeted under the M&E section) as part of the

larger QoC surveys conducted biannually to ensure malaria commodities are reaching intended beneficiaries. *($300,000)*

2. **Strengthen supply chain management for malaria commodities at the county, sub-county, and health-facility levels:** PMI will provide support throughout the supply chain to build capacity and structures to ensure data is available and used to quantify malaria commodity needs and plan orders to prevent stockouts at health facilities. Operational and technical activities will focus on improving the organization, management, and security of commodities within health facilities and among the CHVs in select counties; strengthening and managing county systems to order, track, and evaluate commodity distribution from KEMSA and transfer/re-distribute commodities to alleviate supply shortages and avoid expiries; and troubleshooting to identify distribution bottlenecks and gaps. Capacity-building activities at the county level will focus on the health management team, including pharmacists and county malaria control coordinators and will include training and mentoring to strengthen supervisory and decision-making skills for supply chain management, developing and monitoring work plans, and supporting supervisory visits to sub-county health units and health facilities. To improve malaria commodity consumption data reporting via DHIS2 and use of data for decision making, PMI will support commodity management and reporting system orientations and reporting forms and job aids dissemination to health-facility, sub-county, and county levels. *($700,000)*

3. *Strengthen antimalarial drug quality monitoring and surveillance:* PMI will provide technical, strategic, and operational support for expansion of antimalarial drug quality monitoring to the PPB to strengthen their capacity for registration and inspection processes at national and county level. Strengthening county capacity for routine post-marketing surveillance will decentralize pharmaceutical surveillance activities thereby reducing the load on the central level and empower counties to take ownership for drug quality monitoring and procurement of good quality medicines. PMI will also support the NQCL to maintain its accreditation and promote close collaboration with key stakeholders including PPB, KEMSA, health programs and MEDS. To promote institutionalization and sustainability of MQM, PMI will support capacity building activities including training a pool of health personnel as Trainers of Trainers (TOTs) and champions/team leaders for MQM activities. *($300,000)*

5. **Health system strengthening and capacity building**

PMI supports a broad array of health system strengthening activities which cut across intervention areas, such as training of health workers, supply chain management and health information systems strengthening, drug quality monitoring, and NCMP capacity building.

NMCP/PMI objectives
The NMCP continues to provide leadership and coordination to ensure that malaria control services are equitably and efficiently delivered in all health facilities in malaria endemic and epidemic regions of the country. To achieve this, the program has identified key strategies as part of its program management to address health systems challenges, namely: a) to develop and disseminate policy, lobby for legislation and regulations to guide malaria control in Kenya; b) to strengthen capacity for planning, partnerships, coordination and implementation at all levels; and c) to strengthen resource mobilization capacity to improve malaria control financing, and to strengthen procurement and supply management systems for malaria drugs and commodities.

Since the country introduced devolution in 2012 and most of the national functions became devolved to the 47 counties, service delivery has been affected where personnel roles and responsibilities were changed (i.e., some of the NMCP's malaria coordinators were assigned new responsibilities thus affecting supervision and coordination of malaria control activities in these counties). The NMCP together with PMI and other partners work together to promptly address bottlenecks in service delivery and support continuity of services.

Progress since PMI was launched
PMI has continued to support the GoK's health systems by enhancing the technical capacity of NMCP personnel and developing the procurement and supply chain system to more efficiently deliver supplies and commodities to health facilities and assist the program in monitoring its achievements.

The PMI resident advisors work with the NMCP's technical working groups to develop tools and guidelines for the program. This includes assisting in the development of the Global Fund Round 10 concept note, program review of the national malaria control strategy, and the development of the revised KMS 2014–2018. PMI has supported the NMCP to establish and equip 11 sentinel sites with Minilabs® to test the quality of malaria medicines being dispensed to patients in health facilities. In addition, PMI has procured and distributed over 160 microscopes to health facilities in both endemic and epidemic regions of the country

Progress during the last 12–18 months
Capacity Building: Building on work in previous years in M&E capacity enhancement, PMI supported the training of 40 trainers of trainers (TOTs), ten from each of the four selected malaria endemic counties of Migori, Homa Bay, Kisumu, and Kakamega, thus making a total of 60 TOTs. The TOTs trained were composed of the following county coordinators: malaria, laboratory, nurse, clinical officer, pharmacist, and selected sub-county malaria control coordinators. These TOTs will train other personnel and coordinate malaria surveillance activities in the counties.

PMI also supported the establishment of eight county malaria TWGs to coordinate the implementation of malaria prevention and control activities in consultation with other programs and sectors and to develop integrated malaria work plans for the malaria-endemic counties, in addition to the establishment of 14 county supply chain management TWGs to ensure commodity security across the health sector. On quality improvement, PMI supported the training of 148 health workers from Siaya, Busia, and Kakamega counties. The health workers work in teams to provide on-site quality improvement mentorship. The teams are composed of a pharmacist, laboratory technologist, clinician, and a records officer.

Health information systems: PMI has supported the training of 30 national level Health Information Systems (HIS)/ ICT staff on DHIS2/Master Facility List data management, data quality and data use. This is expected to improve oversight of reporting and support for malaria. In addition, over 190 participants from 12 counties were trained, hence increasing the capacity of county health management teams (CHMTs) and facility managers to use the new ICT equipment. The participants were drawn from the CHMT and SCHMT and are responsible for providing oversight of reporting for facility data including malaria.

Health Workforce: PMI has continued to support activities geared towards the development of a health work force that is able to deliver effective and efficient health services for malaria control. Toward this end, PMI supported two national and two county staff to attend an M&E training in Ghana. PMI also supported the organization of the Kenya national malaria forum (KNMF) a forum organized by the

NMCP that brings together program implementers and scientists to share experiences in malaria control. The two-day forum was attended by over 250 participants from MoH sectors, other GoK line ministries, institutions of higher learning i.e., universities, and colleges, private sector, community based organizations and NGOs.

Two FELTP residents are currently assigned to the NMCP and support both national and field activities. As an example of activities, in the last year FELTP residents have participated in the following: (1) monitoring and evaluation of laboratory reporting and quality assurance/quality control (QA/QC) system implementation; (2) training for case management / parenteral artesunate use; (3) technical working groups for case management, surveillance, M&E and OR; (4) planning and initial pre-test training and fieldwork for the 2015 MIS; (5) fieldwork for the QoC surveys; and (6) malaria microscopy refresher trainings at county level.

A FELTP resident gave an oral presentation of his thesis project, "The Availability and Cost of Malaria Medications and Rapid Diagnostic Tests in Drug Outlets in Rural Siaya County, Western Kenya," at the 2014 KNMF in Nairobi, Kenya and presented a poster at the 63rd American Society of Tropical Medicine and Hygiene Annual Meeting in New Orleans, LA, USA. Another FELTP resident has submitted an abstract entitled "Evaluation of Malaria Microscopy Diagnosis Following Implementation of a Quality Assurance Program in Low-Transmission Areas, Kenya – 2014" to the 64th American Society of Tropical Medicine and Hygiene Annual Meeting in 2015. Both residents worked with PMI partners for their thesis projects.

Plans and justification
PMI, in collaboration with other partners and the NMCP, will continue to support the development of technical and managerial capacity of staff both at the national and county levels to ensure that the program meets the core functions in line with the revised KMS. As a result of task-shifting and reduction in technical staff at the national level, PMI anticipates additional capacity development activities will be required at the national level in the short term and at the county level in the short and longer term to ensure adequate program management and technical expertise.

Proposed activities with FY 2016 funding: **($975,000)**

> **1. PMI direct technical support to the NMCP:** Provision of technical support by PMI advisors and specialists to the NMCP. Advisors and specialists will spend a portion of the work week with the NMCP to provide direct technical assistance and support for activities. *(No cost for this support)*

> **2. Other support to NMCP: *($200,000)***
> a. ***NMCP capacity building:*** Improve the NMCP's technical capacity with regard to implementation, management and leadership development through formal and informal training, courses and workshops, supportive supervision, on-the-job coaching, and mentoring. *($120,000)*
> b. ***Attendance of NMCP staff at technical consultative meetings:*** Provide assistance for NMCP program management and technical team members and priority county malaria control coordinators to attend key technical meetings (e.g., Multilateral Initiative on Malaria). Attendees will be expected to make presentations and share key technical updates with TWGs, partners, and stakeholders. *($50,000)*

c. ***Support to TWGs and Malaria Interagency Coordinating Committee****:* As an essential component of the policy, strategy and guideline review and updating process, the NMCP will have to develop new approaches to realign the existing TWGs and Malaria Interagency Coordinating Committee to fit with the new administrative structures established at the national and county levels. Functional and collaborative TWGs and Malaria Interagency Coordinating Committee are essential to monitor and evaluate the progress of malaria prevention and control interventions and inform partners, donors, and stakeholders. *($30,000)*

3. Support for county malaria control programs: PMI will support the county malaria control programs to develop malaria-specific work plans consistent with each county's malaria profile and the revised KMS and M&E Plan. The malaria control coordinators within the CHMTs are expected to provide critical links and communication between the counties and the NMCP. The CHMTs will be responsible for collating and analyzing malaria related information that will be used in planning for the county's need in terms of carrying out quantification for drugs, laboratory supplies and also planning for the training of more health workers in areas where capacity gaps have been identified. The county teams will also be responsible for organizing review meetings with teams from the sub-counties to assess progress made in each of the counties malaria control interventions. These activities will be carried out in the eight high burden malaria endemic counties in the former Western and Nyanza provinces. The malaria control coordinators will be responsible for ensuring that all malaria control related information is forwarded to the NMCP in time through the appropriate channels. PMI expects to support the CHMTs through existing partnerships to provide technical assistance and managerial and leadership development similar to that at the national level. *($400,000)*

4. Support CHMTs and SCHMTs for quality improvement activities: PMI will support quality improvement activities both at the county and sub-county levels by working with the technical teams (CHMTs and SCHMTs). In order to ensure quality improvement in service delivery in counties and sub-counties, PMI will initially work in three (Siaya, Kakamega, and Busia) of the eight malaria endemic counties in Western and Nyanza provinces. In 2017, the activities will be scaled up to three more counties. In each of these counties, a malaria technical working group has already been constituted to oversee improvement in case management and other malaria indicators. PMI will continue supporting these technical working groups. Furthermore, in the last year PMI supported quality improvement teams in ten high caseload facilities in each of the three counties leading to considerable improvement in case management indicators. With FY 2016 funding, PMI will support the county technical working groups to roll out quality improvement to all health facilities for greater impact. The teams will be trained in identifying service delivery gaps in their facilities especially around case management and supply chain management. The teams will then develop work plans to address the identified service challenges or gaps. The work plans will include steps that will be used to address the challenges and how the challenges will be monitored as the teams carries out its improvement strategies. This approach will ultimately ensure improved data quality, minimize irrational use of drugs and improve its application for decision making i.e. quantification, budgeting and national reporting. Further, two learning sessions will be conducted in each of the counties to document working ideas in detail and package them for scale-up to other high burden counties. *($300,000)*

5. Support FELTP: Provide support for one malaria-focused FELTP resident for the full two-year training program. FELTP graduates are increasingly important as devolution proceeds and staff trained in epidemiology are scarce at the county level to coordinate and lead malaria prevention and control activities. A number of FELTP graduates are now in health leadership roles in the counties, which has increased support for the program and the focus on using data to drive decisions. The budget for each trainee includes tuition and fees, stipend, laptop, books and equipment, a field project, travel, supervision, and administration. *($75,000)*

Table 8: Health Systems Strengthening Activities

HSS Building Block Addressed	Technical Area	Description of Activity
Health Services	*Case Management*	• Strengthen the capacity of laboratory and health care workers in 200 facilities in two endemic counties for malaria diagnostics, microscopy and RDTs through refresher trainings, supportive supervision and on-the-job training • Support and facilitate a refresher training of 79 quality assurance officers on malaria diagnostics from two endemic counties • Support on-the-job training, mentoring and supportive supervision of county/sub-county/health facility staff to improve management of uncomplicated and severe malaria
Health Workforce	*Health Systems Strengthening*	• Support quality improvement activities with CHMTs and SCHMTs in three counties across all health interventions • Continue with the sensitization and orientation of CHVs on MIP messaging and interpersonal communication for increased uptake of ANC services • Train 600 CHWs on Community Malaria case management in prioritized community units in 5 counties
Health Information	*Monitoring and Evaluation*	• Improve oversight of reporting and support for all health facility datasets including malaria by training 30 national level HIS/ ICT staff • Improve data quality and comparability by supporting the development of draft standardized data/ performance review tools and templates which will standardize data and performance reviews across all levels to ensure malaria data among other datasets is reviewed uniformly • Improve performance reporting by supporting 12 malaria endemic and epidemic-prone counties to

		develop Annual Health Sector Performance Reports • Support of HMIS (DHIS2) and IDSR data for production of quarterly surveillance bulletins • Support surveillance training and follow-up, on-the-job mentoring on data use • Support Mini Quality of Care survey in the three counties for comparison with the national quality of care survey
	Operational Research	• Support 2 FELTP master students to evaluate a surveillance system and carry out malaria epidemiology research studies.
Essential Medical Products, Vaccines, and Technologies	*Case Management*	• Support the case management TWG in forecasting, pipeline monitoring, procurement planning for malaria commodities, and use of data for decision making to reduce stock outs at the national and peripheral levels • Continue to support the functioning of TWGs to oversee commodity management in 14 high burden counties • Support the redistribution of malaria commodities from non-endemic to endemic and epidemic regions to prevent expiry of stocks and the availability of medicines where they are needed
Essential Medical Products, Vaccines, and Technologies	*Post-market surveillance of antimalarial medicines*	• Support expansion of antimalarial drug quality monitoring by PPB to strengthen capacity for regulation and inspection at national and county level • Carry out sampling and testing using Minilabs® at 11 sites • Support refresher training, conducted by Minilab® team leaders, as part of sustainability of the MQM program with participants from the 11 sentinel sites
Leadership and Governance	*Health Systems Strengthening*	• Support TWGs across the technical areas and Malaria Interagency Coordinating Committee at national level • Continue to support the Malaria Control TWGs in 8 endemic counties to coordinate the implementation of malaria control activities in consultation other sectors, and to spearhead the development of malaria control work plans for these counties

6. Behavior change communication

NMCP/PMI objectives

The NMCP carried out a mid-term review of its malaria control strategies in 2014. The BCC strategy aims at increasing the utilization of all malaria control interventions to at least 80% by 2018. As a cross-cutting intervention, BCC activities target all malaria control interventions undertaken by the program namely, malaria in pregnancy (MIP), case management, vector control, surveillance and M&E. An advocacy, communication, social mobilization (ACSM) TWG with representation from each of the intervention areas was established to coordinate the development, production and dissemination of all BCC materials and tools.

The NMCP will continue to expand the community strategy, which provides an opportunity for CHVs to use interpersonal communication (IPC) skills at the household level. When CHVs make household visits to assess the health needs of families, they are also able to identify and discuss the reasons for not using ITNs consistently and promote positive health behaviors and malaria prevention messaging. CHVs also discuss identified issues with the Community Health Extension Workers (CHEWs) during the monthly review meetings and these are collected and used to inform future BCC/IPC campaigns and activities.

Progress since PMI was launched
Since 2008, PMI/Kenya has supported training opportunities for malaria program staff on BCC, the production of guidelines, reprinting of 20,000 copies of the malaria treatment guidelines for use in training health workers, and education and communication materials on different aspects of malaria control for World Malaria Day.

In the last two years PMI has focused BCC activities at the community level through CHVs and local organizations. This approach allows for more interpersonal interactions with the beneficiaries of the various malaria control tools.

Progress during the last 12–18 months
In 2014, PMI continued its support to NMCP's BCC activities at the national, county, and community levels. BCC activities undertaken have primarily focused on ensuring that the highest-risk groups are aware of, have access to, and consistently use the available malaria prevention and control tools. With the mass net distribution in endemic and epidemic regions of the country, the ACSM TWG coordinated the development of communication and promotion materials for the campaign. The materials produced included posters, banners, T-shirts, and voucher cards for net redemption. In addition, radio and TV announcements on the campaign were aired on national and county broadcasting stations to raise awareness and inform beneficiaries on how they can access the mosquito nets.

In the three targeted malaria endemic counties of Western and Nyanza Provinces, PMI supported intensive community-based interventions through small group sessions and IPC at the household level to promote the consistent use and maintenance of ITNs and prompt diagnosis and treatment of malaria. The IPC activities were targeted to the highest risk groups in five sub-counties. In these sub-counties, CHVs reached over 297,459 people in almost 293,934 households. In another sub-county, CHVs assisted household members to patch more than 1,308 nets that had small holes by providing patches for stitching on the holes. They also assisted in the hanging of more than 1,387 nets. The wider community was reached through public *barazas* (i.e., community meetings), and local radio and television messaging, interviews, and shows.

In regard to MIP, PMI leveraged the community health strategy supported by a PEPFAR-funded integrated health service delivery platform. CHVs registered over 3,400 pregnant women (64% of expected pregnancies) in one sub-county of Bungoma County in the first quarter of 2014. Of these women 3,094 (91%) received IPTp1, 2074 (61%) received IPTp2, and 1,462 (43%) received IPTp3.

Three Peace Corps volunteers supported PMI in carrying out BCC activities together with the NMCP, county malaria control coordinators, CHEWs, CHVs, and community-based organizations. By June 2014, they had reached a total of 60,000 people with malaria prevention and control messages.

Unfortunately, during the last quarter of 2014, the Peace Corps volunteers were recalled from Kenya for security reasons.

At the national level, PMI supported the production of information, education, and communication materials for use during the World Malaria Day events hosted by counties. The NMCP held the national World Malaria Day event in Busia County in 2015. The day was president over by the Cabinet Secretary for Health. The event was covered by both local and national media. Malaria messaging was included in the main national newspapers and on several national and local radio and television channels.

Like all activities, BCC activities have been affected by the devolution process. In some counties, staff previously leading BCC activities have been assigned new roles thus negatively impacting the continuity of BCC activities. PMI and NMCP are working together with the county governments to ensure that there is a team at the county level that is able to coordinate and build the capacity of county staff to carry out malaria control BCC activities. County teams comprised of key county health management focal persons have been trained on how to plan and implement county specific malaria BCC activities under the leadership of the county malaria control coordinators. However, the GoK has failed to pay community health workers a monthly stipend, which has led to a renaming of community health workers to community health volunteers (CHVs). In only a minority of counties has the community health strategy been included in the health plans and budgets. Most counties continue to rely on development partners to fund stipends for CHVs; however, as U.S. Government and other donor funding declines, the huge recurrent costs for stipend support of a government function are expected to end. It remains to be seen if counties will prioritize funding for the community health strategy going forward.

Plans and justification
In FY 2016, BCC activities will continue to focus at the community level where the community health strategy remains a viable platform for delivering malaria prevention and control messages in endemic and epidemic counties. Other traditional channels of communication will also receive PMI support to ensure that other groups are reached with malaria prevention and control messaging via radio, television and print media.

Proposed activities with FY 2016 funding: **($1,000,000)**
1. **Integrated community-based BCC:** PMI will support the expansion of community-based BCC efforts by increasing outreach to priority populations in endemic counties through different strategies and channels of communication. Enhanced IPC delivered via the community approach will be one of the main channels of communication at the household level. In health facilities, particularly ANC clinics, women's groups, health talks, poster and information displays, and IPC during consultations will be used to deliver malaria messaging. Community *barazas,* dramas, and public gatherings will also be used to deliver malaria prevention and control messaging, including promotion of correct and consistent use of ITNs, early and regular ANC attendance by pregnant women to increase the proportion of women receiving IPTp, and early and appropriate health-seeking behavior and prompt diagnosis and treatment for all persons with fever. *($900,000)*

2. **National BCC promotion and material production:** PMI will support national-level BCC message development and dissemination of key malaria interventions related to the new policies and guidelines. PMI will work with other partners, donors, and stakeholders to coordinate advocacy-related activities, including regular ACSM TWGs and other ad hoc review meetings to monitor and evaluate progress towards malaria control targets. *($100,000)*

7. Monitoring and evaluation

NMCP/PMI objectives
The NMCP's goal is to have all malaria surveillance, monitoring and evaluation, and program indicators routinely monitored, reported and evaluated in all counties by 2018 as included in the revised KMS 2014–2018. In conjunction with revision of the KMS, the NMCP also revised the M&E Plan 2014–2018 to accommodate the new county structure.

Since 2009, the NMCP and stakeholders have relied on a comprehensive national M&E Plan to enable transparent and objective monitoring and evaluation of malaria control activities. The costed M&E Plan is used for M&E advocacy, communications and resource mobilization. Kenya has a large number of stakeholders, including governments, universities, research institutions, private sector, non-government organizations and donor agencies, organized into a Surveillance and M&E TWG that meets on a quarterly basis to provide a forum for discussion, coordination and dissemination of findings of the M&E activities.

The NMCP implements most malaria M&E activities through funding from the Global Fund, PMI, and WHO/DfID. Available funding is targeted towards achieving:

- Improved functioning of M&E unit resources (e.g., technical capacity, hardware and software capability, and information collection, analysis, reporting and dissemination)
- Coordination of malaria M&E activities within the country
- Improved data flow to/from all levels of the health system
- Data quality assurance
- Data use for decision making

PMI's support to M&E in Kenya aligns with the revised M&E plan. Sources of data and information will include the routine health information system, integrated disease surveillance system, periodic household and facility surveys, and activity reports from the implementing partners.

Progress since PMI was launched
PMI has supported data collection activities in Kenya through the routine health information system and periodic household surveys, supporting the 2008–2009 DHS, 2010 MIS, 2014 DHS, and 2015 MIS. PMI provided support to strengthen routine malaria-specific reporting in DHIS2, which started in 2010, to ensure malaria indicators were included in the reporting modules and to develop a malaria commodity module with the NMCP for inclusion in DHIS2. Standard malaria indicators are reported at the facility, sub-county and county levels on a monthly basis. In addition, PMI has provided support over the years for M&E capacity building for the NMCP, including support to attend international M&E courses and holding an M&E course in Kenya for MOH staff at all levels of the health system and Kenya National Malaria Forums in 2011 and 2014.

Progress during the last 12–18 months
The malaria surveillance systems in Kenya include HMIS and IDSR. The NMCP uses data from both DHIS2 and eIDSR in generating the quarterly surveillance bulletins. IDSR has laboratory data (slide and RDT positivity rates), which is missing from DHIS2. The lab data in DHIS2 is limited (<10% reporting). PMI support for surveillance activities included supporting the surveillance curriculum development which focuses on DHIS2 and IDSR data. PMI supported the implementation of the national surveillance training based on WHO surveillance guidance in the eight high burden malaria

endemic counties in western Kenya and Global Fund supported the training in the remaining counties (to be completed by the end of 2015). The surveillance curriculum has been used to train healthcare workers on malaria surveillance, including threshold setting in epidemic-prone areas. Training of 40 TOTs and 649 health workers on malaria surveillance was conducted in four endemic counties with PMI support; this was out of a total of 208 TOTs and 2,091 health workers trained across the country in 2014/2015. By the end of 2015, an additional 40 TOTs and 480 health workers will be trained with PMI support and an additional 1,440 health workers trained with Global Fund support to complete the trainings. PMI supported the technical assistance for quality control of all surveillance trainings including the Global Fund-supported trainings in seasonal and low-malaria transmission areas.

A quarterly malaria surveillance bulletin was developed and distributed by the NMCP to malaria stakeholders in Kenya with PMI support. Over the past year, responsibility for preparing the malaria surveillance bulletins transitioned to the NMCP, with PMI supporting technical assistance as needed. The bulletins include the malaria indicators recommended by the WHO surveillance guidance, standardized graphs, and updates on key activities. PMI has provided support to assist the endemic counties to develop malaria surveillance bulletins and county malaria profiles. PMI also supported the analysis and writing for the NMCP's third annual report.

PMI supported the customization of the routine data quality audit tool for malaria and supported a national data quality audit in 2014, which included malaria datasets. While reporting rates have improved, there still remain issues with data quality. PMI support will be focused to improve laboratory reporting, inpatient reporting, and data quality in the coming year.

PMI provided support for the malaria module in the 2014 DHS survey. The Key Indicator Report was recently released and results are reported in the strategy section. PMI provided approximately 60% of the support for the 2015 MIS, with additional funding from the Global Fund and WHO/DfID. Training has begun and field work will begin in July 2015. The PMI-supported Roll Back Malaria impact evaluation will use the malaria intervention coverage and mortality data from the 2014 DHS survey and planning is underway with the NMCP and partners for implementation in the last half of 2015. The impact evaluation is expected to be completed by mid-2016.

Epidemiologic health facility-based surveillance in former IRS sub-counties (four IRS sub-counties and one non-IRS sub-county, two facilities per sub-county) began in August 2012 with PMI support. Data collection ended in April 2015. Information on suspected malaria cases, RDT test-positivity rate, and the proportion of confirmed cases prescribed an ACT was collected. From February 2013 to December 2014, the testing rate of suspected cases was above 99% across the 10 health facilities. The RDT test-positivity rate for all patients ranged from 37–56% across the facilities, but was highly dependent on seasonality.[30] Three of the five sub-counties have seen an increase in malaria test positivity rate in 2014 compared to 2013. Five bulletins have been developed and disseminated to report the findings from this activity to the NMCP, counties, PMI, and stakeholders. The final analysis, report and manuscript preparations are underway.

PMI continued to support the Quality of Care (QoC) surveys which are conducted on a semi-annual basis and incorporate PMI's standard end-use verification indicators. At least 170 of the approximately 5,000 health facilities were randomly sampled for each survey, for a total of an estimated 340 health facilities sampled per year. The nationally-representative sample includes dispensaries, health centers,

---

[30] MCU, KEMRI, PMI. *Kenya Health Facility-Based Malaria Surveillance Quarterly Project Bulletin.* Kisumu, Kenya: MCU, KEMRI and PMI. December 2014.

and hospital outpatient departments owned by the GoK, faith-based organizations and NGOs across the country. The data from the QoC surveys are referenced frequently to demonstrate program progress and performance. During the past year, two QoC surveys were conducted, the latest in September 2014. Discussions are ongoing around adding indicators to monitor severe malaria treatment given the increased investments and training for injectable artesunate. The QoC survey is currently being conducted at a national level; however, the surveys might transition to county level at some point in the future. PMI will determine if continued support for this type of survey is warranted once plans for county-level surveys are established.

PMI provided support for the second Kenya National Malaria Forum held in October 2014. The two-day event included sessions across the malaria intervention areas and was attended by 250 participants with 50 abstracts presented. PMI staff and PMI's implementing partners provided technical input into the planning of the forum. The NMCP, counties, PMI's implementing partners and FELTP residents all gave presentations to disseminate scientific and programmatic data.

PMI supported technical assistance for the M&E and governance structures including the M&E and OR TWGs. Last year an assessment was conducted of malaria M&E capacity for the NMCP. This past year an M&E capacity building action plan was developed based on this assessment. Technical assistance was provided for the midterm review of the KMS 2014–2018, and the review of the National M&E plan 2014–2018, which are due to be finalized in June 2015. Technical assistance was provided for the Global Fund round 10 reprogramming proposal. PMI also supported the assessment of gender and malaria in Kenya[31] as part of the Global Fund reprogramming and midterm review of the KMS.

Net durability monitoring is underway as part of the 2014/2015 mass ITN campaign. Monitoring will take place in four field sites, each corresponding with one of the four phases of the campaign. Kenya does not procure a single, standardized ITN for mass campaign distributions. Four field sites have been selected because each site corresponds to a different epidemiological zone, different ITN type and manufacturer and different field and housing conditions. The first site (Siaya County) is in a lake-endemic area and has Olyset ITNs procured by NMCP/MOH in 2013, which were delivered in September 2014. The second site (West Pokot County) is in an epidemic-prone riverine area and has Vestergaard ITNs donated by World Vision International with short (<6 mos) expiry dates, which were delivered in November 2014. The third site (Kilifi County) is a coastal-endemic area, has Tianjin Yorkool polyester, circular ITNs procured by NMCP/MOH in 2014, which are planned for delivery in September 2015. The fourth site (Kisii County) is an epidemic-prone highland area, has Permanet ITNs procured by PMI, which are scheduled for delivery in September 2015. Thus far nets have been evaluated in the field and collected for the baseline and 6-month time points for the first two phases in Siaya and West Pokot counties. The third and fourth phases of the campaign will begin later in 2015.

The table below summarizes the available data sources and assessments since 2010 and planned activities through 2018. Note, this table is not exhaustive as there are many additional studies from the demographic surveillance system sites (six in Kenya) and by research institutions.

---

[31] MoH, MCU. *Gender and Malaria in Kenya.* January 2015.

Table 9. Monitoring and Evaluation Data Sources in Kenya, 2010–2018

Data Source	Survey Activities	Year								
		2010	2011	2012	2013	2014	2015	2016	2017	2018
National-level Household surveys	Demographic Health Survey (DHS)					X				
	Malaria Indicator Survey (MIS)	X					X			
	TRaC Survey[a]					X*				
Health Facility and Other Surveys	School-based malaria survey (national and sub-national)[b]	X*	X*							
	SPA survey	X*								
	Service Availability and Readiness Assessment Mapping				X*					
	EUV/Quality of Care survey[c]	X	X	X	X	X	X	(X)	(X)	(X)
	ITN Post-campaign Survey			X			(X)*			
	ITN Post-campaign qualitative assessment					X				
Malaria Surveillance and Routine System Support	Support to malaria surveillance system[d]			X	X	X	X			
	Support to HMIS/DHIS2	X	X	X	X	X	X	(X)	(X)	(X)
	Support to IDSR/eIDSR	X*	X*	X*	X*	X*	X*	(X*)	(X*)	(X*)
Therapeutic Efficacy monitoring[e]	In vivo efficacy testing		X		X		X		(X)	
Entomology	Entomological surveillance and resistance monitoring	X	X	X	X	X	X	(X)	(X)	(X)
Other malaria-related evaluations	Rapid epidemic preparedness and response assessment				X					
	Malaria Program Review/Midterm Review					X				
	Epidemiologic Risk Map & County Malaria Profiles			X				(X)		
Other Data Sources	Malaria Impact Evaluation						X	(X)		

*Not PMI-funded
[a] Aloo, S. Findings of the 2014 malaria TRaC study among populations living in different malarial zones of Kenya.
[b] C.W. Gitonga et al., 2010. Malaria Journal, 9:306; K.E. Halliday et al., 2012. Trop Med Int Health, 17:532; K.E. Halliday et al., 2014. PLoS Med, 11.
[c] End-use verification survey started in 2009 and was incorporated into the Quality of Care survey in 2010.
[d] Health facility-based surveillance in IRS districts, PMI funded. August 2012–April 2015.
[e] PMI-funded TES activities are shown in the table. Additional TES activities were funded by other donors and are not shown.

Plans and justification

With FY 2016 funding, PMI will support the implementation of the revised national malaria M&E plan. PMI will work with the NMCP, counties, and partners to ensure continuity of M&E and surveillance activities. PMI will continue shifting resources to support strengthening of M&E and surveillance at the county level. PMI will support the collection, reporting, analysis, and use of routine malaria data through the DHIS2 at health facility, sub-county, and county levels to enable data-driven decision making.

Proposed activities with FY 2016 funding: **($1,235,000)**

1. **Support the implementation of the revised national M&E Plan:** Continue support for implementation of the revised national M&E plan by providing technical assistance to increase the capacity of existing NMCP M&E staff to ensure that data is used for program improvements. Specific activities are listed below. *($150,000)*

   - Support the NMCP in data collection, analysis, use, and presentation for annual reports, bulletins, and other information products
   - Continue to provide support to implement a national data demand and use plan
   - Support implement of the M&E capacity building action plan including M&E training for NMCP and county malaria and M&E staff

2. **Strengthen HMIS and malaria M&E at county level:** Provide support for strengthening M&E capacity and routine malaria surveillance systems at county and sub-county levels. The national surveillance strategy was rolled out in 2014 and 2015, with surveillance trainings to be completed by the end of 2015. Additional surveillance trainings would be conducted beyond 2015 on an as-needed basis (e.g., attrition, new personnel, poor performers). FY 2016 funding will continue to support mentoring and on-the-job training for data collection and reporting at the CHMT, SCHMT, and facility level with a focus on health facilities with large patient volumes in the eight endemic counties. Technical assistance will be provided during county data review meetings in the endemic counties for increased demand and use of routine data. Reporting completeness and malaria indicators in the DHIS2 system will be monitored longitudinally, by county and facility to monitor the success of these activities. *($500,000)*

3. **Monitoring of interventions:** Support M&E activities for specific intervention areas: *($585,000)*

   End-use verification survey/QoC Survey: Monitor stocks of ACTs and RDTs through the end-use verification survey. The data collection will be done semiannually as part of the QoC survey to allow for a comprehensive evaluation of case management progress and performance. Global Fund provides half of the funding for this activity. *($200,000)*

   Therapeutic efficacy monitoring: Support in vivo drug efficacy monitoring at two sites in western Kenya to complement therapeutic efficacy monitoring studies supported by other partners. *($150,000)*

   Net durability monitoring: Support net attrition/durability monitoring, bioefficacy analysis, and insecticide content monitoring of nets distributed as part of the 2014–2015 mass ITN campaign. Monitoring will take place at four sites, with at least one site corresponding to each of the four phases of the mass campaign. FY 2016 funding will be used to support the year two time point based on PMI guidance. *($225,000)*

4. **Technical assistance—CDC:** Support one CDC in-country visit to provide technical assistance for M&E activities. *($10,000)*

8. Operational research

NMCP/PMI objectives

In March 2015, the NMCP developed a revised list of OR priorities to improve malaria control interventions and programming in line with the revised KMS 2014–2018. The current OR priorities target vector control, case management, MIP, and BCC research questions. In addition, the NMCP has identified research questions related to epidemic response and climate change. In Kenya, OR priorities are set by the NMCP and OR TWG in accordance with the KMS. The OR proposals are reviewed and agreed upon by the OR TWG, which includes PMI representation. PMI fills OR gaps that are identified by the NMCP and are in line with PMI's OR priorities and capacities. In addition to Kenya-specific PMI funding, PMI supports OR studies in Kenya via core funding. Below is a list of the OR studies funded by PMI that have been completed or are ongoing in Kenya.

Progress since PMI was launched

- **Phase III field evaluation of long-lasting insecticide treated nets (Kenya, Malawi, and Senegal).** This multi-year study, completed in May 2014, estimated and compared attrition, physical integrity, and insecticidal activity over time among several brands of long-lasting ITNs, under field conditions in western Kenya. The study found that attrition of nets (which ranged between 30%-40%) was primarily driven by nets being moved, taken, or given away. Findings from this study informed the revision of country specifications for ITNs and how frequently mass net campaigns should be conducted. The results were also used in the initial validation of resistance to damage scores for ITNs which are based upon laboratory textile tests and are designed to predict ITN durability under field conditions.

- **Longevity of insecticides used for IRS.** This study, completed in April 2012, was conducted to determine the optimal insecticide for use after Kenya shifted away from pyrethroid insecticides for IRS. The study identified one formulation of bendiocarb that had the longest duration of efficacy and highest level of acceptance among household owners. Findings from this study were used to inform policy change from pyrethroids to non-pyrethroid insecticides for IRS. Carbamates were recommended but could not be registered due to public health concerns. A single long-acting organophosphate has now been registered for IRS in Kenya.

- **Evaluation of integrated vector control in high- and low-transmission areas of western Kenya.** This study was completed in August 2009. It was conducted to assess changes in the prevalence of parasitemia and anemia after vector control measures were implemented, and estimate the effect of IRS and ITNs on malaria specific outcomes. In this study, ITNs were found to be moderately effective in reducing parasitemia. IRS was highly effective and may have masked the effects of ITNs. These data helped guide PMI and NMCP programmatic decisions and confirmed future commitments to implementing IRS for vector control.

- **Knowledge and adherence to malaria treatment guidelines for pregnant patients in rural western Kenya.** This study, which was completed in December 2013, was conducted to assess the knowledge of malaria treatment guidelines for pregnant women among health care providers and drug dispensers, and to describe their prescribing practices. Results from this study, were presented at the Kenya National Malaria Forum that was held in 2014 and will be discussed at the RBM MIP TWG. Study findings are which are also being disseminated to the wider public health community beyond Kenya, through journal publications and presentations. Findings are being used to develop a package of interventions to address MIP case management in both health facilities and informal drug outlets.

Progress during the last 12-18 months

- **Intermittent screening and treatment (IST) or intermittent preventive treatment (IPT) with dihydroartemisinin-piperaquine versus IPT with sulphadoxine-pyrimethamine for the control of malaria in pregnancy in Kenya: assessment of acceptability, feasibility, and cost-effectiveness within a randomized controlled trial.** This is a multi-year study that began in September 2012. PMI funded the final phase of the study addressing operational feasibility, which was based on the results of the interim analysis from the main trial. The preliminary results of the operational feasibility component will be available in July 2015 and presented at the Roll Back Malaria MIP Expert Review Group meeting in July 2015.

- **Evaluation of intermittent mass screening and treatment to reduce malaria transmission in western Kenya.** This study evaluates the addition of intermittent mass screening and treatment (IMSaT) for malaria to the standard malaria interventions (i.e., ITNs, case management) as a means to further reduce malaria transmission in a high-burden malaria-endemic setting. This is a multi-year study funded through PMI core operational research support. Five rounds of mass screening and treatment in an intervention arm of 27,000 people have been completed to date. The sixth and final round is ongoing as of May 2015. Preliminary data analysis from the first three rounds of IMSaT was presented at the 63rd American Society of Tropical Meeting and Hygiene Annual Meeting in November 2014.

- **Impact of intensification of malaria prevention and control activities on household microeconomics and health service delivery in western Kenya.** PMI core operational research support funded this study. The microeconomic study will determine the economic impact of the intensive malaria-reduction efforts in western Kenya at the household and health-system levels. Study findings will provide evidence on the changes in household income and economic status as measured by wealth quintile as a result of improvements in malaria prevention and control activities. The study will demonstrate any improvements in the efficiency of health service delivery resulting from a decreasing burden of severe and uncomplicated malaria. The study will also provide evidence for the cost implications of malaria-elimination efforts at the county and national levels. The study has started and is expected to be completed in late 2016.

Table 10. PMI Supported Operational Research in Kenya FY 2006–FY 2016

Completed OR Studies			
Title	**Start date**	**End date**	**Budget**
Phase III field evaluation of long-lasting insecticide treated nets (Kenya, Malawi and Senegal)	December 2009	May 2014	~$150,000 (PMI core funding)
Longevity of insecticides used for IRS	September 2011	April 2012	$50,000
Evaluation of integrated vector control in high- and low-transmission areas of western Kenya	May 2008	August 2009	$193,000 (PMI core funding)
Knowledge and adherence to malaria treatment guidelines for pregnant patients in rural western Kenya	August 2013	December 2013	$75,000
Ongoing OR Studies			
Title	**Start date**	**End date (est.)**	**Budget**
Intermittent screening and treatment (IST) or intermittent preventive treatment (IPT) with dihydroartemisinin-piperaquine versus IPT with sulphadoxine-pyrimethamine for the control of malaria in pregnancy in Kenya: assessment of acceptability, feasibility and cost-effectiveness within a randomized controlled trial	September 2012	July 2015	$150,000
Evaluation of intermittent mass screening and treatment (IMSaT) to reduce malaria transmission in western Kenya	January 2013	August 2016	$2,150,000 (FY11–FY13 PMI Core funding)
Impact of intensification of malaria control activities on household microeconomics and health services in western Kenya	January 2015	December 2016	$500,000 (PMI Core funding)

Plans and justification
PMI currently has no studies planned with FY 2016 funding.

Proposed activities with FY 2016 funding: ($0)

9. Staffing and administration

Two health professionals serve as resident advisors to oversee PMI in Kenya, one representing CDC and one representing USAID. In addition, one Foreign Service National (FSN) works as part of the PMI team. All PMI staff members are part of a single interagency team led by the USAID Mission Director or his/her designee in country. The PMI team shares responsibility for development and implementation of PMI strategies and work plans, coordination with national authorities, managing collaborating agencies and supervising day-to-day activities. Candidates for resident advisor positions (whether initial hires or replacements) will be evaluated and/or interviewed jointly by USAID and CDC, and both agencies will be involved in hiring decisions, with the final decision made by the individual agency.

The PMI professional staff work together to oversee all technical and administrative aspects of the PMI, including finalizing details of the project design, implementing malaria prevention and treatment activities, monitoring and evaluation of outcomes and impact, reporting of results, and providing guidance to PMI partners.

The PMI lead in country is the USAID Mission Director. The day-to-day lead for PMI is delegated to the USAID Health Office Director and thus the two PMI resident advisors, one from USAID and one from CDC, report to the USAID Health Office Director for day-to-day leadership, and work together as a part of a single interagency team. The technical expertise housed in Atlanta and Washington guides PMI programmatic efforts.

The two PMI resident advisors are based within the USAID health office and are expected to spend approximately half their time sitting with and providing technical assistance to the national malaria control programs and partners.

Locally-hired staff to support PMI activities either in Ministries or in USAID will be approved by the USAID Mission Director. Because of the need to adhere to specific country policies and USAID accounting regulations, any transfer of PMI funds directly to Ministries or host governments will need to be approved by the USAID Mission Director and Controller, in addition to the US Global Malaria Coordinator.

Proposed activities with FY 2016 funding: **($1,638,000)**

1. **USAID in-country staffing and administration:** Support for one PMI resident advisor and one Foreign Service National staff member to oversee activities supported by PMI in Kenya. Additionally, these funds will support pooled USAID Kenya Mission staff and mission-wide assistance from which PMI benefits. *($978,000)*

2. **CDC in-country staffing and administration:** Support for one PMI resident advisor to oversee activities supported by PMI in Kenya. *($660,000)*

Table 1: Budget Breakdown by Mechanism (Year 9) FY 2016
President's Malaria Initiative – Kenya
Planned Malaria Obligations for FY 2016

Partner Organization	Geographic Area	Activity Description	Activity Budget	Partner Subtotals	%
AIRS Task Order 6	Endemic County(s)	IRS implementation and management	$7,000,000	$7,000,000	22%
ASSIST	Endemic/ Epidemic Counties	Support CHMT and SCHMT for quality improvement	$300,000	$300,000	1%
CDC IAA (Atlanta)	Endemic/ Epidemic Counties	Technical Assistance: CDC TDYs	$29,000	$144,000	0.4%
		Supplies for entomologic monitoring	$10,000		
	Nationwide	Technical Assistance: CDC TDY	$10,000		
		Technical Assistance: CDC TDY	$10,000		
		Technical Assistance: CDC TDYs	$10,000		
		Support one FELTP resident	$75,000		
MalariaCare	Endemic Counties	Provide supportive supervision for malaria diagnostics within the national quality assurance/quality control framework	$400,000	$700,000	2%
		Provide supportive supervision, training, and mentoring for healthcare providers for malaria case management	$300,000		
MCSP	Endemic Counties	Sensitize and train healthcare workers and supervisors on the malaria in pregnancy package of interventions and improve facility reporting	$350,000	$800,000	2%
		Sensitize, orient, and supervise CHVs on malaria in pregnancy package of interventions and improve reporting	$350,000		
		Strengthen national and county level malaria in pregnancy policy and monitoring capacity	$100,000		
MEASURE Evaluation PIMA	Endemic Counties	Support the implementation of the revised national M&E plan	$150,000	$650,000	2%
		Strengthen HMIS and malaria M&E at county level	$500,000		
TBD	Endemic/ Epidemic Counties	Entomological and insecticide resistance monitoring in IRS and other selective areas	$320,000	$1,420,000	4%

		Strengthen supply chain management for malaria commodities at the county, sub-county and health-facility levels	$700,000		
		Support for county malaria control programs	$400,000		
	Nationwide	Strengthen supply chain management for malaria commodities at the national level	$300,000	$1,075,000	3%
		Monitoring of interventions: End-use verification survey/Quality of Care Survey	$200,000		
		Monitoring of interventions: Therapeutic Efficacy Monitoring	$150,000		
		Monitoring of interventions: net durability monitoring	$225,000		
		Support to NMCP	$200,000		
TBD-bilateral	Endemic Counties	Logistic and program support for ITN distribution	$1,500,000	$2,500,000	8%
		Integrated community-based IEC/BCC	$900,000		
	Nationwide	National IEC/BCC promotion and material production	$100,000		
TBD-Supply Chain Contract	Endemic/ Epidemic Counties	Procure ITNs for health facility-based distribution channels	$6,000,000	$14,831,600	46%
	Endemic County(s)	Procure ITNs for alternate distribution channel	$400,000		
	Nationwide	Procure RDTs	$2,560,000		
		Procure AL	$4,571,600		
		Procure severe malaria medications	$1,300,000		
TBD-KEMSA	Nationwide	Provide warehousing and distribution for RDTs, ACTs and severe malaria medicines	$841,400	$841,400	3%
USP PQM	Nationwide	Strengthen antimalarial drug quality monitoring and surveillance	$300,000	$300,000	1%
USAID/CDC	Nationwide	USAID and CDC in country staffing and administration	$1,638,000	$1,638,000	5%
VectorWorks	Endemic County(s)	Support alternate ITN distribution channel	$200,000	$200,000	1%
FY 2016 Budget Total				$32,400,000	100%

Table 2: Budget Breakdown by Activity (Year 9) FY 2016
President's Malaria Initiative – Kenya
Planned Malaria Obligations for FY 2016

Proposed Activity	Mechanism	FY 2016 Budget	FY 2016 Commodities	Geographic area	Description of Activity
PREVENTIVE ACTIVITIES					
Insecticide Treated Nets					
Procure ITNs for health facility-based distribution channels	TBD-Supply Chain Contract	$6,000,000	$6,000,000	Endemic/Epidemic Counties	Fill part of the ITN gap for routine distribution by purchasing up to 1.5 million ITNs. Routine distribution: free-of-charge to pregnant women and children under one through the ANC and EPI/child health clinics.
Logistic and program support for ITN distribution	TBD-bilateral	$1,500,000	$0	Endemic/Epidemic Counties	Provide logistical support, including transportation and storage of nets, for distribution of the 1.5 million ITNs within the national routine distribution system.
Procure ITNs for alternate distribution channel	TBD-Supply Chain Contract	$400,000	$400,000	Endemic County(s)	Procure 100,000 ITNs for an alternate distribution channel.
Support alternate ITN distribution channel	VectorWorks	$200,000	$0	Endemic County(s)	Support an alternate ITN distribution channel in about one county to maintain universal coverage following the start of the 2017/18 mass campaign. The specific approach (e.g., community-based, school-based) will be based on the planning activity funded with FY 2015 funding.
SUBTOTAL ITNs		$8,100,000	$6,400,000		

65

Indoor Residual Spraying

Activity	Mechanism			Location	Description
IRS implementation and management	AIRS Task Order 6	$7,000,000	$3,150,000	Endemic County	Support IRS in one endemic county (estimated to reach 276,000 structures and up to 1.4 million people) with at least 85% coverage in all targeted areas.
Entomological and insecticide resistance monitoring in IRS and other selective areas	TBD	$320,000	$0	Endemic/Epidemic Counties	Continue insecticide resistance monitoring (including resistance intensity) in endemic counties with an IRS program and counties where IRS has been withdrawn. Expansion to selected counties identified as having gaps in insecticide resistance monitoring by the NMCP.
Supplies for entomologic monitoring	CDC IAA (Atlanta)	$10,000	$0	Endemic/Epidemic Counties	Purchase supplies to support entomologic monitoring activities.
Technical Assistance: CDC TDYs	CDC IAA (Atlanta)	$29,000	$0	Endemic/Epidemic Counties	Support two visits from CDC to provide assistance in implementing IRS activities.
SUBTOTAL IRS		**$7,359,000**	**$3,150,000**		

Malaria in Pregnancy

Activity	Mechanism			Location	Description
Sensitize and train healthcare workers and supervisors on the package of malaria in pregnancy interventions and improve facility reporting	MCSP	$350,000	$0	Endemic Counties	Target all healthcare facilities that provide ANC services in five counties. An estimated total of up to 500 healthcare facilities will be reached. Activities will include the orientation and training of facility in-charges and health service providers on the MIP package and ANC data collection, and implementation of a quality improvement framework for healthcare facilities providing ANC services.

Activity	Implementer			Location	Description
Sensitize, orient, and supervise CHVs on malaria in pregnancy package of interventions and improve reporting	MCSP	$350,000	$0	Endemic Counties	This activity will include the orientation, training and supervision of CHVs to increase early referral to ANC services and to register all pregnant women for follow-up. CHVs are trained to undertake BCC activities and to refer and track pregnant women to ensure that they receive IPTp at health facilities. An estimated 5,500 CHVs will be sensitized and oriented using the community strategy and other innovative community approaches. The target is to reach approximately 50,000 women of reproductive age with community MIP messages and services.
Strengthen national and county level malaria in pregnancy policy and monitoring capacity	MCSP	$100,000	$0	Endemic Counties	Support will be provided at the national and county levels for policy and monitoring of MIP-specific activities. Technical support will be provided to counties on MIP as necessary.
SUBTOTAL MIP		**$800,000**	**$0**		
SUBTOTAL PREVENTATIVE		**$16,259,000**	**$9,550,000**		
CASE MANAGEMENT					
Diagnostics and Treatment					
Procure RDTs	TBD-Supply Chain Contract	$2,560,000	$2,560,000	Nationwide	Procure and distribute up to 8 million RDTs to help fill the gap at level 2 and 3 health facilities (dispensaries and health centers) and to provide RDTs for the community case management strategy.
Procure AL	TBD-Supply Chain Case	$4,571,600	$4,571,600	Nationwide	Procure and distribute up to 4.5 million AL treatments to fill gaps in the public sector and community case

management.

Activity	Partner			Location	Description
Procure severe malaria medications	TBD-Supply Chain Contract	$1,300,000	$1,300,000	Nationwide	Procure severe malaria drugs, including up to 500,000 vials of injectable artesunate, as needed.
Provide warehousing and distribution for RDTs, ACTs and severe malaria medicines	TBD-KEMSA	$841,400	$0	Nationwide	Provide warehousing and distribution for RDTs, ACTs and severe malaria medicines from central to facility level nationwide. KEMSA, the central medical store, transitioned from quarterly "push" supply system to an order-based (i.e., "pull") system from counties due to devolution.
Provide supportive supervision for malaria diagnostics within the national quality assurance/quality control framework	MalariaCare	$400,000	$0	Endemic Counties	Activities will include strengthening capacity of laboratory and healthcare staff for malaria diagnostics through initial and/or refresher trainings and capacity-building for supportive supervision, on-the-job training, and mentoring at the health facility level. Support operationalization, scale up and integration of QA/QC framework and systems for malaria diagnostics in endemic counties. Conduct monitoring and evaluation of QA/QC officer performance and program implementation.
Provide supportive supervision, training, and mentoring for healthcare providers for malaria case management	MalariaCare	$300,000	$0	Endemic Counties	Provide supportive supervision, training and mentoring for malaria case management, including severe malaria, at the health facility level in line with national case management guidelines to promote rational use of medicines.
Technical Assistance: CDC TDY	CDC IAA (Atlanta)	$10,000	$0	Nationwide	Support one CDC TDY to provide technical assistance for malaria diagnostics.

Activity	Implementer			Location	Description
Technical Assistance: CDC TDY	CDC IAA (Atlanta)	$10,000	$0	Nationwide	Support one CDC TDY to provide technical assistance for malaria case management.
SUBTOTAL DIAGNOSIS AND TREATMENT		$9,993,000	$8,431,600		
Pharmaceutical Management					
Strengthen supply chain management for malaria commodities at the national level	TBD	$300,000	$0	Nationwide	Support the NMCP and KEMSA to strengthen supply chain management and build capacity to ensure commodity data are available (through DHIS2) and used to accurately forecast and quantify commodity needs at the national level and prevent stockouts at all levels of the health system. Areas of technical and operational support to KEMSA will include warehousing, financial management, information systems and monitoring and evaluation of performance.
Strengthen supply chain management for malaria commodities at the county, sub-county and health-facility levels	TBD	$700,000	$0	Endemic/Epidemic Counties	Support throughout the supply chain (county, sub-county, and health-facility levels) to build capacity and structures to ensure data is available and used to quantify commodity needs and plan orders to prevent stock outs. Activities will focus on improving the organization, management and security of commodities within regional and county warehouses, strengthening county systems to order, track and evaluate commodity distribution from KEMSA and transfer/redistribute commodities to alleviate supply shortages and avoid expiries.

Activity	Partner	Budget	Budget	Location	Description
					Supervision of stock monitoring, on-the-job training and collection of antimalarial drug consumption data. Assist with distributing job aids and materials to health facilities.
Strengthen antimalarial drug quality monitoring and surveillance	USP PQM	$300,000	$0	Nationwide	Strengthen antimalarial drug quality monitoring through the provision of technical, strategic and operational support to the NMCP, drug monitoring sentinel sites in the counties, Pharmacy and Poisons Board, and National Quality Control Laboratory.
SUBTOTAL PHARMACEUTICAL MANAGEMENT		$1,300,000	$0		
SUBTOTAL CASE MANAGEMENT		$11,293,600	$8,431,600		
HEALTH SYSTEM STRENGTHENING / CAPACITY BUILDING					
Support to NMCP	TBD	$200,000	$0	Nationwide	Provide technical assistance and capacity building to improve the NMCP's capacity to fulfill the roles and responsibilities in line with the revised KMS. Provide support for technical working groups and inter-agency coordination committees for robust participation and regular meetings.
Support for county malaria control programs	TBD	$400,000	$0	Endemic/Epidemic Counties	Programmatic support to malaria control coordinators, county pharmacist, county lab coordinator, disease surveillance coordinator, and health management teams at the county and sub-county levels to increase supervision and management capacity for program implementation. Support emerging malaria control issues at the

Activity	Mechanism			Geographic Area	Description
					county level. Assist with inter-county coordination.
Support CHMT and SCHMT for quality improvement	ASSIST	$0	$300,000	Endemic/Epidemic Counties	Support quality improvement activities with CHMTs and SCHMTs, to improve program performance across all malaria intervention areas.
Support one FELTP resident	CDC IAA (Atlanta)	$0	$75,000	Nationwide	Support one FELTP trainee for the two-year program to increase epidemiologic capacity within the MOH. PMI encourages the MOH to second FELTP graduates to the NMCP or endemic/epidemic counties to enhance the capacity of malaria control programs. The budget for each trainee includes tuition, stipend, laptop, materials, training and travel for the two-year program.
SUBTOTAL HSS & CAPACITY BUILDING		$0	$975,000		
BEHAVIOR CHANGE COMMUNICATION					
Integrated community-based IEC/BCC	TBD-bilateral	$0	$900,000	Endemic Counties	Expand community-based IEC/BCC efforts by increasing outreach to priority counties and at-risk populations, particularly pregnant women and children less than five years of age, through different strategies and channels of communication, such as IPC. Messages and mode of dissemination will be dependent on the

Activity	Partner/Mechanism			Location	Description
					venue and target group but will include health facilities, ANC clinics, home visits by CHVs, *barazas*, and public gatherings.
National IEC/BCC promotion and material production	TBD-bilateral	$100,000		Nationwide	Support national-level IEC/BCC message development and dissemination on key malaria control interventions; donor coordination; advocacy-related activities, including regular review meetings with malaria partners, donors, and stakeholders to monitor and evaluate program progress. Activities will also strengthen the Division of Health Promotion.
SUBTOTAL BCC			**$1,000,000**		
MONITORING AND EVALUATION					
Support the implementation of the revised national M&E plan	MEASURE Evaluation *PIMA*	$150,000		Nationwide	Increase data demand and use of routine data for programmatic improvements at national level. Continue support for implementation of the revised national M&E plan by providing technical assistance to increase the capacity of M&E staff and to ensure that data is used for decision making.

Activity	Partner	Amount		Location	Description
Strengthen HMIS and malaria M&E at county level	MEASURE Evaluation *PIMA*	$500,000	$0	Endemic Counties	Increase data demand and use of routine data for programmatic improvements at county level. Support for M&E strengthening at the county level, working with the CHMT, SCHMT and high volume health facilities. Continue capacity building in counties for surveillance and M&E activities, mentorship, and reporting in line with county malaria control plans.
Monitoring of interventions: End-use verification survey/Quality of Care Survey	TBD	$200,000	$0	Nationwide	Monitor quality of care for malaria case management and assess stockouts through the End-use verification tool included in the biannual Quality of Care surveys.
Monitoring of interventions: Therapeutic Efficacy Monitoring	TBD	$150,000	$0	Nationwide	Support in vivo drug efficacy monitoring in 2 sites, complementing the TEM activities of other implementing partners.
Monitoring of interventions: net durability monitoring	TBD	$225,000	$0	Nationwide	Continue net durability monitoring for a third year in 4 sites. Net attrition/durability, bioefficacy analysis and insecticide content monitoring will be conducted on nets distributed in each the four phases of the 2014–2015 mass ITN distribution campaign.
Technical Assistance: CDC TDYs	CDC IAA (Atlanta)	$10,000	$0	Nationwide	Support one CDC TDY to provide technical assistance for M&E activities.
SUBTOTAL M&E		**$1,235,000**	**$0**		
IN-COUNTRY STAFFING AND ADMINISTRATION					
USAID in-country staffing and administration	USAID	$978,000	$0	Nationwide	USAID staffing and mission-wide support costs

73

CDC in-country staffing and administration	CDC IAA (Atlanta)	Nationwide	CDC Advisor staffing and support costs
	$660,000	$0	
SUBTOTAL IN-COUNTRY STAFFING	**$1,638,000**	**$0**	
GRAND TOTAL	**$32,400,000**	**$17,981,600**	

www.ingramcontent.com/pod-product-compliance
Lightning Source LLC
Chambersburg PA
CBHW081239280526

45787CB00006B/2723